MIDDLE EASTERN COOKERY

MIDDLE EASTERN COOKERY

SUZY BENGHIAT

ARTUS BOOKS
LONDON

NOTE

1 All recipes serve four unless otherwise stated.

2 All spoon measurements are level.

3 Metric and imperial measurements have been calculated separately. Use one set of measurements only as they are not exact equivalents.

4 Preparation times given have been calculated from recipe testing and indicate the average time a cook might expect to spend; adjust the time accordingly if you are a beginner or a very experienced cook.

5 Cooking times may vary slightly depending on the individual oven. Dishes should be placed in the centre of the oven unless otherwise specified.

6 Always preheat the oven or grill to the specified temperature.

7 If a certain dish can be prepared in advance to a certain point, this has been indicated in the recipe with an asterisk (*).

Shown on this page: Apricot Petits Fours, Konafa and Baklava, (*recipes on pages 128 and 130–1*), traditionally served with tiny cups of strong black coffee.
Previous page: Fila Pastry Borek with Spinach Filling and Spiced Carrots (*recipes on pages 35 and 88*), served as *mezze* with bread rings, *crudités*, olives and feta cheese.

To Pa, Monique and especially Fred
for their loving and sustained support

First published in Great Britain in 1984 by
George Weidenfeld & Nicolson Limited
91 Clapham High Street
London SW4 7TA

Reprinted 1993, 1994

Artus Books, Orion House, 5 Upper St Martin's Lane,
London WC 2H 9EA

ISBN 1 85605 164 1

Phototypeset by Keyspools Limited, Golborne, Lancs
Printed in Italy

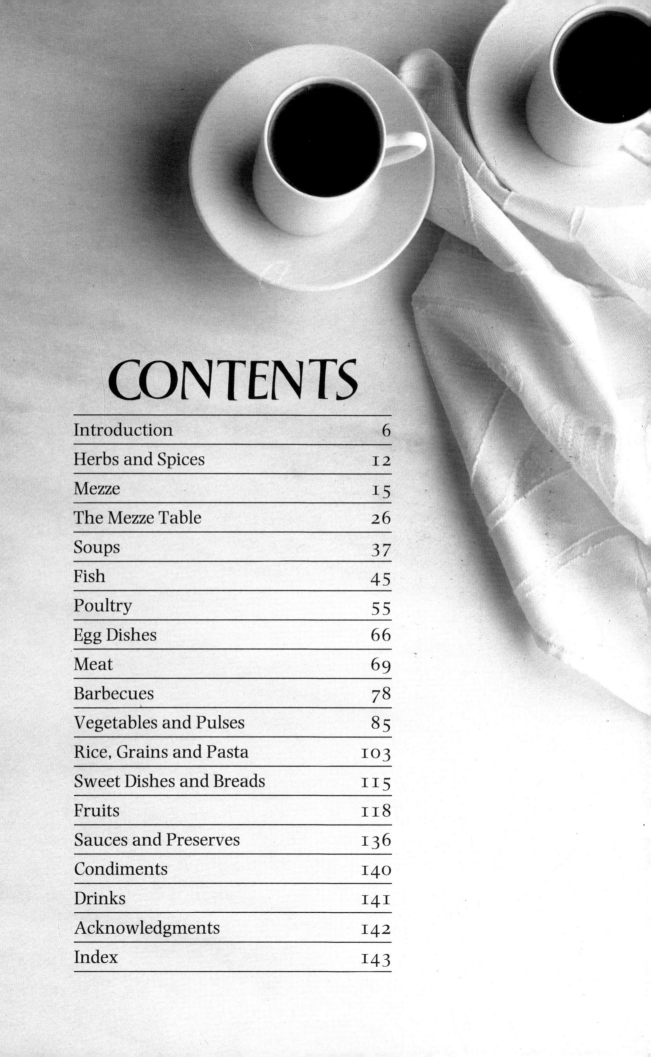

CONTENTS

INTRODUCTION

The choice of dishes in this book is the fruit of over thirty years of cooking experience and constant research and innovation. My experience began long before I myself learned to cook. It is rooted in Cairo, where I was born and spent all my early years before I came to settle in London with my parents and brother.

In fact Egypt, especially the Egypt of my childhood, is a very good starting point for learning about the cookery of the vast, amorphous area which is loosely described as the Middle East. Throughout history, the country has been a crossroads of many civilizations, a fact reflected in the composition of its population in the 1930s and 1940s. In the large cities, people of various origins, religions and nationalities had been living side by side for generations, forming an integral part of Egyptian society yet keeping their own cultural identity and customs. This complex mosaic of groups was loosely defined not only by nationality – native Egyptian, Italian, British, Greek or French – but also by religious tradition and language. Muslim, Jewish and Christian communities embraced the different nationalities, and everybody spoke the local Arabic dialect, French and any of several other languages. Only the British community stood rather stiffly aside. A strong Turkish influence also lingered from the time of the Ottoman occupation, though without much actual Turkish presence. I myself went to the French Lycée, while my brother went to the English School, and we enjoyed a multitude of national and religious holidays.

Cooking is as much a means of expression as language and of course each nationality kept its own way of

Melons on sale by the Caspian Sea, the world's largest landlocked body of water, bordered by Iran and the Soviet Union. The Caspian is the world's richest source of the finest grey-black caviar, the tiny roe of sturgeon which are treated by salting. Each year, Iran harvests more than 200 tons of caviar, a delicious – and expensive – delicacy, usually eaten as an *hors d'oeuvre*.

cooking. Yet just as language is alive and changing, so eating habits and tastes were also exchanged and shared. Food in Egypt therefore included elements from the whole range of what is usually thought of as Middle Eastern fare, but also with a strong Italian influence. There were charcoal-grilled kebabs, *koftas* (meat balls) and fish, with various accompanying dips; savoury pastries of different kinds, filled with cheese, meats and vegetables, then fried or baked; stuffed vegetables, poultry and fish; rice, couscous and other grain dishes; stews combining meats with fresh vegetables or pulses; sweets, puddings and pastries with nuts and dried fruits, flavoured with rose or orange flower water, or sometimes with mastic, which was also used as a chewing gum. The *mezze* tradition was important, and meals generally composed of a large assortment of dishes were put on the table for each person to choose from, rather than a rigid number of courses in the western way. My mother made dishes mainly of an Italian type. Both she and my paternal grandmother also provided Spanish Sephardic specialities and we also ate food of Syrian and Lebanese origin – all of these strongly influenced by Turkish cooking – as well as North African and Greek and others peculiar to the Jews of Egypt. Most important of all was the strong sense of hospitality and generosity that is a feature of the whole region.

As a child, I had limited tastes. I avoided most soups and cooked vegetables, and sweet things other than ice cream. But even within these limitations I had an enormous range to choose from. Within Cairo's small Jewish community there was much diversity resulting from the migration of peoples. What I liked best of all, however, was the real Egyptian Arabic food of the people: *foul* (beans), *falafel* and fried fish bought from street vendors, or cooked by the servants for themselves on days when the menu was too European for their taste. In the afternoons I used to slip away from my homework and visit the kitchen to sample their leftovers, which probably explains how I got my preference for cold food!

Years later, I began cooking under the guidance of my mother in London. My nostalgia for Egypt led me to try, with the *naïveté* of a beginner, to reproduce what I hoped would be the exact flavour of the tahina dip of a famous popular restaurant or of the kofta in tomato sauce made by our old cook Fatima. Eventually I did achieve some measure of success; and some dishes here are hardly altered from those I ate as a child. But my choice of recipes for this book is also governed by the way my own cooking has evolved. With increasing experience I have learned both to be more adventurous in my tastes, and to develop my own style. I have also gained a more realistic view of what a regional or national speciality is, in part as a result of travelling and meeting people from different parts of the world, and in part because the western interest in ethnic foods has produced a plethora of books – some excellent, some not – which have revealed often quite unexpected similarities. Thus I have come to realize that a dish we considered typically Egyptian might well be of Turkish origin and found in countries as far apart as Yugoslavia and Tunisia; in the same way I have also discovered many genuinely Egyptian dishes that were unknown to my family. It has also become clear how within one country – particularly one where transport and communications were undeveloped – there is often great diversity between the cooking of the big cities and that of different regions. Here traditions are handed down from mother to daughter, and each family evolves its own style.

There are dishes here that I have gradually adapted, sometimes under the influence of other cuisines. For instance, I cook vegetables by the traditional method of simmering them in a sauce, but the example of Chinese food has taught me to cook them very lightly so that they are still crisp. I have made certain changes, such as reducing the amount of fat in a dish or replacing butter with sunflower oil, for dietary or health reasons.

One prevailing myth that I would like to dispel here is the notion that Middle Eastern food is some kind of key to good health. It is healthy enough, simply because it uses fresh produce and freshly prepared rather than manufactured convenience foods, and because it is well balanced with plenty of vegetables, often raw, and pulses, nuts and fruits, with rather limited amounts of meat, but that is all. If people in the Middle East escape many of the ailments of western society it is principally because they live simply and cannot avoid at least some strenuous exertion. Those who lie about, overindulging themselves with butter, oil and sugar – whatever the cuisine – are prone to exactly the same cardiovascular diseases as westerners.

I am presenting here dishes as I cook them in London, taking advantage of today's wealth of ingredients from all over the world, and of modern kitchen equipment, especially the food processor. Other dishes I have cooked on holiday, perhaps in a caravan or beach hut, using a single frying pan. Some call for careful planning, others can be improvised in minutes. In a deliberate effort to avoid any mystique about 'authentic' ways of cooking, presenting or eating Middle Eastern food, the presentation of the dishes in the photographs has been left as it might be seen through western eyes.

All these dishes represent different aspects of Middle Eastern cooking; but I have deliberately avoided an academic, comprehensive survey of the food of individual countries. With only a few exceptions I have not ascribed a particular location to a dish.

The names, too, of dishes and ingredients have been chosen in a very arbitrary manner, since each dish is known under many names in the diverse languages of the Middle East. Anyway, the exotic-sounding names given to a dish in different regions often all translate to some prosaic term such as 'stew'.

Often it is the vessel in which food is cooked that gives it its name, as with the *tajine*. This word for the typical North African earthenware pot with a conical lid has an Egyptian equivalent, *tagen*, which, however, means a wide metal saucepan. The well-known Moroccan and Algerian *tajines* are essentially stews; but those of Tunisia are more like rich omelettes, a kind of cross between an omelette and a soufflé similar to the *eggah* of Egypt, the *kuku* of Iran, the 'Spanish omelette' or the Italian *frittata*.

To confuse things further, different names are used in one country for the same dish. What is called *falafel* in Cairo is known in Alexandria as *'ta'meya'*; *melokheya* in Egypt means a leafy plant used for a green soup while in Algeria and Tunisia the word is used to mean the pods of okra, which only a botanist would recognize as a distant member of the same plant family. Their relationship is shown only by the fact that both have a slightly glutinous texture – and, incidentally, both have long been favourites of mine!

I have chosen names either because they are the ones most commonly used in Britain; or because they refer to a specific dish in one country; or, where neither of these reasons applies, I have generally used the dish's name in colloquial Egyptian Arabic.

FOLLOWING THE RECIPES

Real cooks do not cook in the way in which most cookery books are written, and it is hard to reduce to mere words an activity which relies on taste, smell, sight, skill, judgment and common sense, not to mention creativity – especially when writing for a generation of readers who are accustomed to following a recipe word for word as if it were a knitting pattern. I have tried to come to a satisfactory compromise by giving quantities according to the current convention in the ingredients lists while often at the same time making it clear in the instructions that the cook has quite some leeway. I allow that an accurate ingredients list is a necessary guide for the first time one cooks a dish, and in particular for the inexperienced cook; but I believe that I have also given enough information about how things should look or smell, or how flavours develop, to give you confidence to use your initiative. To me, terms such as 'a pinch', 'a touch of', or 'walnut-sized' are quite accurate enough when you rely on your own senses and judgment rather than precise measurements.

Total quantities should also be taken only as a rough guideline not only because people's appetites vary but also because the amount one needs of each dish varies with the number of dishes offered. Both with *mezze* or 'appetizers' and in the substantial part of a Middle Eastern meal there are usually a number of dishes to choose from. The recipes here are, unless stated, for four portions when served in a conventional western way; but obviously if you have two meat and two vegetable dishes, served with rice and salad, there should be enough for more people.

As to the time it takes to prepare a dish, average preparation times are given for each recipe as a very rough guide. You will notice that the cooking time is generally included in the total, and this is because of the way I cook and teach; this is also reflected in the way the instructions have been written. For example, in making a stew, sauce or soup which includes chopped onions, other vegetables and meat I do not cut everything up before beginning to cook it. While the chopped onions are softening on a low heat in oil or butter, you can safely get on with trimming the meat and preparing the other vegetables, adding these to the pan as they are ready, starting with those that take longer to cook. This saves a lot of time. Remember too that preparation time depends on your skill and experience. I

Weighing out olives at a Greek grocery in London. In recent years, Middle Eastern food stores have become a familiar sight in cities up and down the country, offering cooks a wealth of ingredients – from vine leaves to *melokheya*, fila and konafa pastries and ready-spiced coffee – and a source of inspiration.

can stuff a couple of dozen vine leaves in less than an hour without hurrying, but the first time you try this it will take you much longer.

This leads me to more general advice on how this book, or indeed any cookery book, should be used. Read it first: leaf through the recipes, including the introductions and other notes. This will give you a much sounder basis for success than measuring all the ingredients and lining them up in neat little piles before you have read the method properly.

If Middle Eastern cooking is unfamiliar to you, it is probably best not to attempt to prepare a whole meal of dishes you have never cooked before for an exotic dinner party to impress your guests. It is much better to start by making the simpler dishes, using only one or two new ingredients, and to try them out on your family before you move on to more complicated things. A good example of this would be Persian Chicken with Rice (see page 63) which includes an unusual garnish of caramelized orange peel. First master the method for Persian Rice with a Crust (see page 106), and perhaps also try out the caramelized peel as a garnish for something else so that you can be sure that it poses no problem. After that, this spectacular dish is very easy to make.

I realize that a lot of the advice given above and in the cooking tips in various parts of the book – for example, on choosing the right size of saucepan, or on making soft breadcrumbs, or on frying or grilling – are superfluous to good cooks. But they have been prompted by my experience as a cookery teacher as they have proved useful to a number of my students – and not only to the least experienced among them.

TRADITIONAL AND MODERN EQUIPMENT

Most of the cooking described in this book is done on top of the stove, mainly because this is how I have always done it myself. Many of the dishes can be cooked in the oven if you prefer, but I find it easier to control the speed of cooking and in particular the amount of liquid by using a saucepan. Many of the dishes need simmering and long, slow cooking. That is why it is so important to use a heavy-based pan. The shape of the pan is important too: it is generally best to use a wide pan except, of course, for making soups.

No utensil does everything. Thus, for example, I like to use a pressure cooker only for certain specific purposes. The cooking of foods that require a very long time can be speeded up in this way – but only up to a point. For example, when cooking *foul* (beans), I'd give them perhaps 25 minutes under pressure, but then release the pressure and simmer them half-covered for some time afterwards. Only in this way can the full flavour develop.

For grilling indoors, I find ordinary cooker grills, whether gas or electric, less effective than grilling over a hot ring. Dry foods such as peppers, aubergines or corn on the cob can be put on a wire-mesh heat diffuser – the type normally used under saucepans, and which has replaced the old, dangerous asbestos mats. A heavy, ridged cast-iron grill pan, with a non-stick coating if you like, is ideal for grilling meat, poultry and fish. The grill pan must be very hot indeed before the food is put on it. If the food to be grilled is without fat and has not been marinated in oil, the grill pan should be first heated, then lightly brushed with oil immediately before the food is put on. Grill the first side of the food for just long enough to sear it, then turn it over and treat the other side in the same way. If the food then needs more cooking (this will depend on its size and whether you like things well done) lower the heat to medium. When the food is cooked remove it and pour a little marinating liquid, wine or water on to the grill pan and scrape. It will sizzle and reduce, absorbing the scraps and juices on the grill pan to make a tasty sauce.

I began using a steamer for food that is traditionally cooked in this way, such as couscous – and some Chinese dishes – and since then I have found it invaluable as a way of reheating many foods without drying them out. Most Middle Eastern dishes can be reheated very successfully

The most popular sweetmeats of the Middle East, Baklava and Konafa, may be sampled ready-made from specialist patisseries and grocers. Here sweet and savoury pastries are traditionally baked, in vast round trays, and cut into bite-sized portions.

Many local street markets now supply much of the produce needed in Middle Eastern and Indian cooking. At this stall, vegetables which are common to a number of classic cuisines – courgettes, peppers, French beans, chicory, artichokes, mangetout and aubergines – jostle with small 'Cyprus' cucumbers and fresh coriander – two essentials of Middle Eastern cookery.

this way, to the extent that it is often worth while making more than you need at the time, and storing some in the refrigerator or freezer.

I also like to use a Chinese wok for deep or semi-deep frying. It uses much less oil than conventional pans.

A blender or, even better, a food processor, is a real boon. Without my processor I should never have started making some of the traditional Middle Eastern dishes that require long, tedious and exhausting work, such as Kibbeh (see page 110) and the minced fish dishes (see page 52). It is also useful for chopping large amounts of parsley or fresh coriander leaves, and for making *do'a* (see page 140).

FREEZERS AND MICROWAVE OVENS

A freezer can be used to store Middle Eastern dishes in exactly the same way as any other food. Stews, soups and pastries all freeze excellently. Where any dish in this book is best frozen at a particular stage, or needs any other special treatment, I have added a note to the recipe. Otherwise, follow the advice in your freezer handbook.

Certain types of dish can be cooked in a microwave oven – again, consult the handbook – but not those whose flavour depends on browning the ingredients, or on slow cooking; and nothing that is meant to be crunchy. However, a microwave oven is useful for the quick thawing of bulky frozen dishes such as stews and soups; I would only use one for this purpose.

SPECIAL FLAVOURINGS AND INGREDIENTS

The speed at which new and exotic ingredients are now being introduced and becoming widely available makes a list like this very quickly obsolete. Anyone who lives in a city or large town with a cosmopolitan population is well placed to find almost any unusual food. Visits to local markets, Asian and Middle Eastern food stores, health food shops and larger supermarkets should soon show you what there is to be had locally. But however great the variety available, do not think that you must have a large number of exotic ingredients to cook in a Middle Eastern style. In fact, unless you are already familiar with this kind of cooking, I would advise you to start by using ingredients, herbs and spices that you already know. You may well have met many of them in Indian cooking.

Herbs and spices Those used in Middle Eastern cooking are illustrated on pages 12–13. I think that cumin seed, coriander seed, turmeric and chilli would give you a good basis from which to start. After that you might try cardamom, ginger, and perhaps fenugreek (though personally I don't like this, and you won't find it in this book).

Other characteristic flavourings include sesame seeds and roasted almonds. Each gives a crunchy texture and nutty flavour to all kinds of dishes, and both are a very good way for vegetarians to supplement their diet.

Acid fruits Another distinctive flavour in Middle Eastern food comes from lemons and other sour fruits. To my taste, limes are incomparably the best. They are expensive if bought in ordinary shops; but many Asian shops sell small limes, often by weight, for little more than lemons. I find that even a small lime can give more juice than a large but thick-skinned lemon. Other acid flavours come from dried apricots and pomegranate seeds. These need to be soaked before use, and the soaking water is included in the recipe: see, for example, those for stuffed vegetables (see pages 92–5) or Lahme bi Ajeen (see page 30). Tamarind may be used in the same way. Living in England, I have found that rhubarb is a marvellous alternative to lime juice for stuffed vegetables.

Dried limes are by far my most exciting discovery, made a few years ago. I had not known of these in Egypt. They were given to me by a French friend married to an Iraqi, who called them *lamoun Basra*. Since then I have found that they are used in other parts of the Middle East, and you can get them in England; they are imported from Pakistan. You can add them whole to a stew and they will soften as it cooks so that you can cut them up and eat them with it; or while still dry they can be crushed to powder and added like a spice. They also make delicious hot drinks (see page 141).

Rose and orange flower water can be interchanged as you like, as delicate flavourings for fruit dishes, puddings, and various other sweets. It is advisable to buy them from Middle Eastern food shops rather than chemists. The best brands come from Cyprus, and there is also a lovely French kind which is sold in dark blue bottles.

Mastic or mastika is a resin used for flavouring milk puddings and a famous Turkish ice cream, Dondurma Kaymak (see page 120). In Egypt it is also added with other spices and herbs to chicken broth. It should be used in very small amounts, and crushed with sugar or salt. A piece the size of a small pearl will flavour at least 1 litre or 2 pints of milk. It is better to use only a little at first, taste and add more if necessary. Too much imparts a bitter flavour.

Mastic is widely used as chewing gum. It has a flavour reminiscent of pine resin. When it becomes too dry to chew, it is softened by mixing it with shavings of wax. The best mastic is imported from the Greek island of Chios.

Burghul or pourgouri is sometimes loosely termed 'cracked wheat', but it is not the same as the plain cracked wheat available from health food shops. It has been cooked and dried before crushing. It is eaten in the same way as rice, or in salads, or as the basis of the classic Lebanese Kibbeh (see page 110).

Kishk or trahanas The first is the Egyptian name, the second the Greek Cypriot one, for cracked wheat cooked with yoghurt or soured milk, then dried in the sun. It is sold either in granular form or in small sticks. It is used to thicken soups and sauces, and gives a delicately acid flavour.

Tahina or tahini This is sesame-seed paste. It is sold in jars (do not use dark tahina), and forms the basis of dips and sauces. Some kinds of *halva*, a popular sweet, are made from tahina.

Samna or smen is a clarified, slightly sour butter used particularly in Egypt and North Africa. In the recipes here I have substituted clarified butter, made by heating ordinary butter very gently to evaporate the water in it, or a mixture of oil and butter; you could also substitute ghee, available from Indian shops.

Oil Although olive oil is also widely used in Middle Eastern cooking, I prefer to restrict its use to dishes which require its special flavour; where the type of oil is not specified in the recipes, I would use sunflower or corn oil.

Vinegar In my experience, wine vinegar is not much used in the Middle East and I find that its distinctive flavour sometimes clashes with other ingredients. You will see that my usual salad dressing is made with lime or lemon juice rather than vinegar. For dishes that do call for vinegar, such as Higado con Vinagre (see page 73) and Zemino (see page 136), use a good distilled malt vinegar – but not the highly coloured and caramelized type.

Fila and konafa pastries These two types of pastry are widely used all over the Middle East and are available in Britain from some supermarkets as well as Middle Eastern shops. They are both made only from flour and water, and fat is added at the time of use. Fila pastry comes in ultra-

The date harvest in the Tafilalet Oasis in Morocco. Dates are a mainstay of the diet in many parts of the Middle East. Fresh dates, served on their own or with nuts, make a simple but luscious end to any meal. Dried or fresh, they form the basis of a number of classic puddings and pastries.

thin, tissue-like sheets. It can be made at home by very skilful and patient cooks, but it is usually manufactured commercially. Konafa looks like white shredded wheat and is always bought ready-made. Both are now often made by large-scale factory processes, but they are still also made by hand in some areas; I have recently seen this done with great panache both in Cairo and in Alexandria.

The fila maker is called a *fatayri*. He rolls and stretches the dough by throwing it into the air and passing it from hand to hand with incredible speed. You may have seen pizza dough makers doing something similar; but fila is far thinner and each sheet is much wider. The completed sheets are cut to size, and filled and fried to order on the spot.

The konafa maker is even more skilful, and breath-taking to watch. He has in front of him a huge, round heated tray. On his right is a bowl full of thin batter. He holds a perforated ladle, though some konafa makers disdain such an aid and use their fingers. He takes some batter and very swiftly dribbles it across the tray. The moment the batter hits the tray it sets into something like extra-fine white vermicelli. At once, before it starts to colour, he gathers it up with his left hand and adds it to a pile on a table. Meanwhile his right hand is already pouring the next batch of batter.

Konafa is sold in Britain vacuum packed, often frozen. Instructions for handling it are given on page 131.

When fresh, fila is easy to handle and should be soft and pliable. But even then, its thinness and lack of fat allow it to dry out quickly so that it becomes brittle. When using fila flat in large pieces, as you would for Baklava (see page 130) or for chicken or meat pies, this does not matter. However, it can be prevented from drying out by keeping it well covered and moist until you use it. Further instructions are given in those recipes in which fila is used.

I hope that this book will give people who do not know Middle Eastern cooking a good general appreciation of it. I also hope that readers who cook these dishes will not follow the recipes slavishly, but will adapt them as a basis for experiment.

Harvesting peanuts in Anamur, on the southern coast of Turkey. The Middle East as a whole produces nuts of all kinds, and they form an intrinsic part of the region's cooking, both savoury dishes – sauces, stuffings and pilafs – and cakes, biscuits and pastries.

In the Middle East, where some form of refreshment is an essential part of any social visit or business transaction, time-honoured rituals for the making and serving of coffee – distinctively rich, dark and strong – are observed to this day. Here, the green coffee beans are roasted in a long-handled iron pan over an open fire, before being pulverized, briefly boiled and served in the traditional tiny cups without handles. Instructions for making and serving coffee in the Middle Eastern way are given on page 141.

Personally, I feel flattered when someone tells me that a recipe I gave them turned out perfectly; but I am more deeply pleased when they say that they have been using my dressing for their own salads, or my short pastry for their quiches and Cornish pasties, or that they made their Christmas mince pies with fila pastry in coils like borek. I would like people to use this book as a source of inspiration to widen their everyday repertoire. In particular, vegetarians should find exciting ways to vary their diet, not only from the Vegetables and Pulses chapter but also by adapting dishes from the other sections.

As for those who are already familiar with Middle Eastern cookery, and even Middle Eastern cooks themselves, I hope that they will find ideas for variations on a well-loved dish, even if they are convinced that their own special version of other dishes cannot be improved.

CHOOSING THE RIGHT SAUCEPAN

It is very important to use a saucepan of the right type and size for a particular dish.

Weight Especially for dishes that are cooked slowly, a heavy-based pan is essential. When buying a pan, make sure you are not misled by one with a heavy handle only. Stainless steel is a very poor conductor of heat, and a pan of this metal must have a thick copper bottom; this does not apply to cast-iron or aluminium pans.

If you have to use a pan with a base that is not heavy enough, the defect can be largely overcome by setting it on a wire-mesh heat diffuser, which works on both gas and electric stoves. Asbestos mats are a health risk and should not be used.

Size Inexperienced cooks often use too small a pan and pile the ingredients up so that the food at the top remains uncooked while that at the bottom burns. I have worked out the following reliable rules. When cooking on top of the stove, the saucepan should be small enough for the ingredients to completely cover the bottom, and large enough for all the ingredients not to fill it more than half full. If you choose a pan of the appropriate size, you will find that my instruction to line the base of the pan with oil will automatically give you the amount needed.

FRYING

The quantity of oil you use for any method of frying is entirely a matter of depth, and thus varies with the size of the pan. The following is an explanation of the terms I use in this book.

Shallow frying or sautéing The oil should just coat the base of the pan when it is poured in and swirled around.

Deep frying The food that is being fried should be completely submerged in oil, and covered to a depth of about 2 cm [¾ in.].

Semi-deep frying There should be a fair amount of oil, but it need not cover the food. Here you have to turn the food over to brown it evenly. For frying in this way it is a great help to use a wok: it needs much less oil than a flat-bottomed pan. Anything that is deep fried in the recipes can be semi-deep fried provided that you turn it, but not vice versa.

HERBS AND SPICES

Herbs, spices and condiments are an essential part of both savoury and sweet Middle Eastern dishes. Good cooks seldom decide in advance exactly which and how much of each they will use: they taste at different stages of cooking. She or he knows how flavours develop as the food cooks, or after it has cooled if it is to be eaten cold.

Herbs are used fresh or dried, and spices are bought whole or ready-ground; dried herbs or ready-ground spices must be used while still fresh and not allowed to go stale. Often the dried product has a quite different taste from the fresh one and sometimes, as with dried mint and dried root ginger, this is preferable. Some spices, notably coriander, caraway and cumin seed, are roasted before use to develop the flavour. Traditionally, cooks in the Middle East have bought their spices from the special spice section in the market, where they can find them roasted to the exact degree they require, and freshly ground. The spice sellers, the best of whom attract a faithful clientele, also make up their own blends. For western cooks, who cannot buy freshly roasted spices, it is better to buy spices whole, and roast, grind and blend them at home. Heat them in a small frying pan without oil, shaking the pan continually until you smell the fragrance developing. A pestle and mortar is ideal for grinding small quantities of spices; you can also grind them in a small electric grinder.

In all the recipes in this book which include parsley, the flat-leafed variety is infinitely preferable. Like fresh coriander, it is generally available from Middle Eastern food shops and markets. To store any that you do not need at once, wash it thoroughly, dry it very well and cut off the stems, reserving them. Chop the leaves finely and put them in a plastic box in the freezer. They will stay separate, so when you need the herb for flavouring you can just take a handful straight from the frozen box and throw it in. I also keep the stems in the freezer and use them, tied in bundles, to add flavour to soups and sauces.

1 Dill weed 2 Saffron
3 Oregano 4 Flat-leaved
parsley 5 Pomegranate seeds
6 Paprika 7 Black peppercorns
8 Mastic 9 Tamarind slices
10 Cumin seed 11 Nutmegs
12 Dried lemons and limes
13 Mint 14 Sea salt
15 Caraway seed 16 White
cardamom pods 17 Green
cardamom pods 18 Fennel
seeds 19 Cinnamon sticks
20 Ground ginger 21 Chilli
powder 22 Sumac
23 Coriander seed
24 Turmeric 25 Allspice
berries 26 Fresh coriander

MEZZE

Mezze might be translated as 'appetizers', 'hors d'oeuvres' or 'snacks'. But such words in no way convey the range of delicacies, cooked and uncooked, which fall into that category; and, more important, they do not give the full flavour of the way of life common to all Middle Eastern countries in which they play a part.

I firmly believe that it is impossible to learn about or judge the food of a country or region only through restaurants. Yet in this case I would say that the best and quickest way to introduce someone to the food of the Middle East is to treat them to a *mezze* meal in a Greek, Lebanese or Turkish restaurant. There are several reasons for this. An enormous variety of fare is offered, up to twenty different items, all in small portions. They range from the familiar *crudités*, served with exotic dips and cubes of cheese, to more unusual items: rissoles, grilled or fried, with or without sauces; grilled prawns or chicken livers; small pasties made of different pastries with various fillings, baked or fried. In fact any dish of sufficient taste and interest can be presented as a *mezze* if it is small or can be served in small portions. Thus in one sitting one can get quite a good idea of the range of the region's food.

This diversity reveals something else about Middle Eastern food. Other dishes are presented in the same way, not as a limited set number of courses served in a sequence and with each course calculated to feed a given number of people. Instead, the food is usually spread out on the table, there is a greater variety of dishes and people help themselves, choosing dishes with contrasting flavours and textures – but certainly not piling things up into an indiscriminate jumble.

Three typical dips for the *mezze* table (*left to right*) Bessara, Hummus Dip and Tahina Dip, with a bowl of crunchy Fried Dried Broad Beans (*top*)

15

TAHINA DIP

PREPARATION TIME
10 minutes

1 clove garlic
salt
30 ml [2 tbsp] tahina paste
juice of 1 lemon, or to taste

TO GARNISH
a few sprigs parsley, chopped

(picture on page 15)

This thick sesame seed paste, known under various spellings, is eaten both as a dip in its own right and added to other dips. One popular combination is Hummus bi Tahina (see below), a dip made with chickpeas. I prefer tahina on its own, diluted and flavoured in the most traditional Egyptian manner as described here.

1 Crush the garlic with salt in a mortar. Stir the tahina well so that the oil on top blends with the thick part at the bottom of the jar. Add the tahina to the mortar if it is large enough, or put both the tahina and garlic into a bowl. Stir well.
2 Add the lemon juice gradually, stirring all the time. The colour and texture will change: don't worry, just keep stirring until all is thoroughly mixed. Add some water a little at a time, stirring each time until it is completely incorporated before adding more. The paste should now be slightly thicker than double cream and even in colour and consistency.
3 Taste, and add more lemon juice if necessary – it should taste quite lemony. When you are satisfied, stir in a little more water until the tahina is as thick as double cream or mayonnaise. Serve in shallow bowls, garnished with chopped parsley.

I sometimes add a pinch of ground cumin, or a little vinegar as well as the lemon juice. But I never add any oil. Tahina is in itself an oily paste, and in fact often replaces oil when added to other dips.

Tahina Dip should be stored in a bowl covered with cling film, to prevent it drying out. However, if it does, just mix in a little water or lemon juice.

HUMMUS DIP

PREPARATION TIME
8 hours soaking
1 hour 30 minutes, including
    1 hour 10 minutes cooking

120 g [4 oz] chickpeas
1 medium onion
1 clove garlic or more, to taste
20 ml [4 tsp] olive oil
2.5 ml [½ tsp] turmeric
salt to taste
juice of ½–1 lemon, to taste

(picture on page 14)

This plain but agreeable dip made from chickpeas is popular all over the Middle East, and is becoming more and more popular in Britain too. I like to brighten the taste by cooking the chickpeas with some flavouring: turmeric imparts a subtle aroma and also gives the beige paste a more attractive colour.

1 Wash the chickpeas and leave them to soak in plenty of water for 8 hours.
2 Discard any floating debris and remove the chickpeas, reserving the water. If necessary, peel the chickpeas by rubbing them between your hands.
3 Chop the onion and garlic and soften them over medium to low heat in enough oil to just line the base of the pan. When the onion is transparent, stir in the turmeric and a little of the soaking water from the chickpeas. Add the chickpeas and cover with enough of the soaking water to reach about 3 cm [a good 1 in.] above the level of the peas. Bring to the boil, then simmer until done, about 1 hour. If you use a pressure cooker, add enough water to reach 5 cm [2 in.] above the peas and cook for only 25 minutes.
4 When the chickpeas are soft, drain them and reserve the liquid. Mash them with a fork and add a little liquid. Then purée them with a food mill to the consistency of thick mayonnaise. (If you have a liquidizer or food processor, there is no need to mash the chickpeas first.)
5 Transfer to a bowl and add salt, lemon juice and the remaining oil, tasting and mixing to get the right balance. You might like some more garlic. If so, crush the garlic with salt, add a little of the hummus, mix well and scrape out into the larger bowl.

HUMMUS BI TAHINA This well-known and delicious variant is made simply by replacing the oil added at the end with a tablespoonful of tahina paste.

> PEELING DRIED CHICKPEAS
> This is much easier than it sounds. After they have been soaked, just rub the chickpeas between your hands and return to the soaking water. The peel will float to the surface and can be easily discarded.

BESSARA (BROAD BEAN PURÉE)

PREPARATION TIME
8 hours soaking
2 hours, including 1¾ hours
  cooking

120 g [4 oz] peeled dried broad
  beans
2 spring onions
1 clove garlic
15 ml [1 tbsp] chopped fresh
  coriander
5 ml [1 tsp] crushed dried mint
5 ml [1 tsp] ground cumin seed
salt and pepper to taste
a dot chilli powder (optional)

TO SERVE
1 medium onion
olive oil for shallow frying
1 clove garlic
15 ml [1 tbsp] crushed
  coriander seed

(picture on page 14)

Bessara is a purée made from dried broad beans and herbs. It is traditionally garnished with Ta'leya (see page 140), a dressing of garlic and fried crushed coriander seed. Use ready-peeled broad beans.

1 Wash the beans and leave them to soak in plenty of water for 8 hours.
2 Discard any loose floating bits of skin and pour off the water. Transfer the beans to a saucepan. Add water to about 3 cm [1 in.] above the tops of the beans, and bring to the boil.
3 Chop the spring onions (both white and green parts) and a clove of garlic. When the beans are boiling skim off any froth. Add the onions and garlic, and stir. Bring back to the boil, half cover and lower the heat to simmer. Stir from time to time, and add more water if necessary. The beans should be soft in about 1½ hours. If you use a pressure cooker, cover the beans with 6 cm [over 2 in.] of water and cook for about 25 minutes.
4 Purée the mixture in a food mill or a food processor, return to the pan and continue cooking. It should have a purée consistency: if it is too liquid, leave the pan uncovered so that it dries out.
5 Add the fresh coriander, mint, ground cumin, salt and pepper to taste and, if you like, a little chilli powder. Stir well, taste and adjust the seasoning. Leave to cool.
6 For the garnish, slice the onion into rings and fry in hot olive oil until brown and crisp. Remove from the pan and reserve. Chop the garlic very finely. Pour away most of the oil, leaving just enough to gently fry the garlic and the crushed coriander seed until it gives off a sweet smell – be careful not to burn it. Serve the Bessara in a fairly shallow dish, with the Ta'leya and onion rings on top.

Bessara is also served with separate olive oil, lemon wedges and extra chilli powder or sauce, to allow people to adjust the seasoning to their own taste.

FRIED DRIED BROAD BEANS

PREPARATION TIME
8 hours soaking
5 minutes, including cooking

120 g [4 oz] peeled dried broad
  beans
salt
oil for deep frying

(picture on page 14)

These crunchy, golden-brown beans are eaten in the same way as salted roast nuts.

1 Wash the beans, cover in plenty of water and leave to soak for 8 hours.
2 Discard any floating skin, drain the beans, peel them if necessary, roll them in salt, then dry with kitchen paper.
3 Heat oil in a deep fryer until quite hot. Use a large slotted spoon to fry the beans a few at a time. Lower them very slowly into the hot oil and fry until golden brown. Drain them on kitchen paper, and eat cold.

Chickpeas can be deep fried and eaten in exactly the same way.

Radishes and spring onions are often served with other raw vegetables as part of a *mezze* spread. RIGHT Huge radishes and spring onions on sale at the Yemenite market in Tel Aviv, the largest city in Israel.

FALAFEL

Falafel are small bean, chickpea or lentil rissoles eaten with Tahina Dip (see page 16) as a 'mezze', or in pitta bread with an Egyptian-type salad. They form part of the staple diet in Egypt, where they are often eaten with Foul Medames (see page 100), which in fact are made with the same small brown bean that is my favourite for these rissoles. However, the beans need to be peeled after soaking, which can be a tedious job. I therefore recommend using a larger dry broad bean which is sold ready peeled and has a similar flavour.

PREPARATION TIME
8 hours soaking
2¾ hours, including 2 hours resting and 10 minutes cooking

250 g [8 oz] dried broad beans
15 ml [1 tbsp] very finely chopped parsley
15 ml [1 tbsp] very finely chopped fresh coriander
4–5 spring onions
1 clove garlic
2.5 ml [½ tsp] ground cumin seed
salt and pepper to taste
a small pinch bicarbonate of soda (optional)
oil for semi-deep frying

1 Wash the beans and soak them in plenty of water for 8 hours.
2 Remove any floating bits of skin. Drain the beans, dry them with kitchen paper or a cloth and grind them in a mincer, using the fine disc, or in a food processor. The beans should have the consistency of a fairly dry, slightly grainy purée.
3 Mix the chopped herbs with the beans in a bowl. Finely chop the green part of 4 or 5 spring onions with a clove of garlic. Add these to the mixture with the ground cumin, a little salt, pepper, and bicarbonate of soda (if used). Knead well. Taste and adjust the seasoning. (Don't worry, it is quite nice raw.) The mixture will have a lovely pale green colour, speckled with dark green. Leave the paste to rest, uncovered, in the refrigerator for a couple of hours to dry out. This will make it easier to mould.
4 Damp your hands slightly. Take a piece of paste the size of a large marble. Knead it in your palm and form it into a ball (see page 77). Put this on a plate or tray and flatten it slightly with your finger. Make all the paste into rissoles in this way.
* Falafel may be prepared in advance to this stage and kept in the refrigerator or freezer. Freeze loose on a tray, then pack in bags. Fry straight from the freezer.
5 Pour oil into a frying pan so that it is at least 3 cm [1 in.] deep, or use a wok if you have one. Heat the oil and fry the rissoles, turning them until they are golden brown on both sides. If they begin to turn dark brown, lower the heat. Put the cooked Falafel on kitchen paper to absorb some of the oil.

You can also make larger Falafel to eat in a sandwich or as part of a snack lunch. Use walnut-sized pieces of paste. As each rissole expands in the hot oil, flatten it to make sure it cooks through.

LABAN CHEESE BALLS

1 litre [1¾ pints] thick natural yoghurt
10 ml [2 tsp] salt
coarsely ground black pepper, crushed dried mint or paprika

(picture on page 27)

1 Add the salt to the yoghurt and strain it through fine muslin. Tie the muslin into a bundle and leave excess moisture to drain out over the sink or a bowl for a day or two. (In this form it can be spread on bread and sprinkled with chopped fresh mint or wild thyme.)
2 Leave the cheese to dry in the refrigerator, roll into small balls and store in a jar of olive oil. When you want to eat them, remove, drain and roll in the pepper, mint or paprika.

AUBERGINE PURÉE

This delicious 'mezze' combines different flavours and spices. Choose medium or large aubergines, the long kind rather than round ones if available. They have to be cooked until they are soft inside and rather charred outside. There are two ways of doing this: grilling on top of the stove, using a cast-iron grill pan, or baking in the oven. I prefer the first method because it is quicker. An ordinary grill can also be used instead of the grill pan. (If baking, make two or three slits in the skin before putting in the oven.)

PREPARATION TIME
45 minutes, including 15 minutes salting and 20 minutes cooking

3 medium or 2 large aubergines
salt
1 clove garlic
½ small onion
lime or lemon juice to taste
15–30 ml [2 tbsp] olive oil
30 ml [2 tbsp] chopped parsley

1 Wash and dry the aubergines. Put the grill pan on the stove. If the aubergines are large, start grilling them at medium heat, turning them frequently until they begin to soften. Then turn up the heat and continue grilling and turning until the skin is charred all over and broken in places. Medium aubergines can be started on a high heat, as they will soften in the time it takes for the skin to char, about 20 minutes.

Aubergine Purée (*back left*) and Falafel, traditionally served with a bowl of Tahina Dip

2 Hold each aubergine carefully by its stem, and split it open lengthways with a sharp knife. Some liquid will ooze out: wait till it stops dripping. Sprinkle the cut surfaces with a little salt and stand the aubergines upright, stem uppermost, in a colander and leave for about 15 minutes. This procedure removes more moisture from the aubergines, improving the texture of the purée. In the past it was also necessary to make the aubergines less bitter, but with those generally available now this is seldom a problem.

3 Crush the garlic with salt and put it in a bowl. Grate the onion into the bowl and mix. A food processor can be used for all the chopping and mixing. Spoon the aubergine pulp out of the rind. Chop the fibrous bits with a sharp knife. Add all the pulp to the bowl.

4 Mix the ingredients thoroughly, add lemon or lime juice and taste. Add more juice or more salt if necessary. Then add the oil very gradually as you would with mayonnaise, stirring the mixture constantly. Stop adding oil as soon as the surface of the purée takes on a shine. Taste again. Stir some of the parsley into the purée. Serve in bowls, sprinkled with the rest of the parsley.

You can vary the seasoning by using vinegar instead of lemon juice, or the two combined. A touch of chilli powder or sauce is sometimes added, or a spoonful of yoghurt. Another seasoning you can add is a T'atbil (see page 140).

BABAGHANOUSH Add 15 ml [1 tbsp] tahina paste instead of the oil.

Fried Aubergine, Onion and Tomato Salad (*left*) and Pepper Salad

PEPPER SALAD

PREPARATION TIME
30 minutes, including 5–10
    minutes cooking
1 hour wait

1 each green, red and yellow
    peppers
1 clove garlic
salt to taste
about 5 ml [1 tsp] vinegar
about 15 ml [1 tbsp] olive oil

TO GARNISH
black olives (optional)

The peppers for this salad are charred to make them more digestible and – more importantly – to improve the flavour. Choose longish peppers rather than round ones if available: they are easier to grill evenly.

1 Wash and dry the peppers. Grill them, turning from time to time until the skin is charred and split on all sides. Put them in a bowl, cover with a cloth and leave to cool. This makes peeling easier.
2 Peel the peppers, cut them open and wipe away bits of charred skin with kitchen paper. Discard the seeds and slice into strips. Arrange them in a shallow serving bowl, chop the garlic very finely indeed and sprinkle it on top. Sprinkle the peppers with salt. Dribble a little vinegar over them, making sure it goes on the salt. Leave for a few minutes until the vinegar has dissolved the salt, then swirl the dish around gently to spread the seasoning all over.
3 Dribble the olive oil all over the surface. Taste, and adjust the seasoning. If possible, leave for an hour or so before serving. Serve garnished with black olives if you like.

For an alternative presentation, chop the peppers very finely, season as above, then arrange them in piles of different colours (see page 55). Garnish with chopped hard-boiled egg whites and yolks. Vary the seasoning by using lime or lemon juice instead of vinegar, or by adding a small touch of chilli sauce or powder.

Some years ago, during a visit to Belgrade, a friend offered me a very similar salad to this pepper one, to 'introduce me to typical Serbian food', not realizing how familiar this kind of dish was to me. However, her version included aubergines, and the flavours blend extremely well. Now I often make Aubergine Purée (see page 18) and this pepper salad separately, then combine the leftovers for the following day.

FRIED AUBERGINE, ONION AND TOMATO SALAD

This is another delicious way of serving aubergines, as an hors d'oeuvre or as a salad to accompany grilled meat or a cold roast, or as part of a vegetarian meal.

PREPARATION TIME
overnight salting
30 minutes, including 15–20
    minutes cooking

2 medium aubergines
salt
4–5 tomatoes, or a 400 g
    [14 oz] can
oil for semi-deep frying
1 large onion
15 ml [1 tbsp] vinegar
1 clove garlic

TO GARNISH
a few sprigs parsley, chopped

1 The night before you want to cook them, prepare the aubergines. Cut off the tops and bottoms and discard. Take thin lengthways strips about 3 cm [1 in.] apart off the peel. (This prevents the slices from buckling up when fried.) Cut the aubergines into slices about 1 cm [⅜ in.] thick. Put the slices in a colander and sprinkle with salt. Cover with a plate, weight it down well and leave for at least 10 hours. If possible, turn the slices over after a few hours and press down again.

2 Take out the slices and dry them by pressing between sheets of kitchen paper. Slice the tomatoes if fresh, or drain canned tomatoes.

3 Pour about 4 cm [1½ in.] depth of oil into a large frying pan. A wok is particularly suitable for this job, because it uses far less oil. The oil should be about 4 cm [1½ in.] deep in the middle. Heat the oil, and test the temperature with a tiny piece of aubergine. When it sizzles to the surface fry the aubergine slices in batches till brown on both sides. As you remove each batch, put it on kitchen paper to absorb excess oil. You may have to adjust the temperature of the oil as you go along.

4 When the aubergines are done, take the pan off the heat and pour the oil through a metal sieve lined with kitchen paper into a metal or other heatproof bowl, so that you can reuse it. Slice the onion into rings. Return 15 to 30 ml [1 or 2 tbsp] of oil to the pan, and reheat till hot but not sizzling. Quickly fry the onion rings until just golden, and put them on another piece of kitchen paper.

5 Make sure the pan is hot, then put in all the tomatoes and squash them quickly so that they are just scorched but not cooked. Remove them and put on a plate. Pour the vinegar into the pan. Bring to the boil, scraping the bottom of the pan with a spoon or spatula, and take off the heat.

6 Arrange the aubergines, tomatoes and onion rings in a shallow bowl. Chop the garlic very finely indeed and spread it all over the salad, then sprinkle evenly with a little salt and dribble the pan juices on to it to dissolve it. The salad probably does not need any added oil. However, the above method of degorging the aubergines is so efficient that it just might. Taste a little and judge for yourself, and adjust the seasoning at the same time. Allow the salad to cool completely, then serve garnished with chopped parsley.

Fried aubergine slices are also delicious just covered with natural yoghurt mixed with a little crushed garlic.

FRYING AUBERGINES

This is an improvement on the classic method of salting aubergine slices to make them absorb less oil in frying. Put the slices in a colander over a bowl, sprinkle them with salt and cover with a plate. Instead of leaving them only 10 minutes, or even 2 hours – which is the longest time usually recommended, leave them for at least 10 hours or overnight. Then dry them with kitchen paper. Although they will have withered, they will recover their shape when fried and you will be astonished at how little oil they take up.

Sweet and hot peppers of many kinds play an important part in all the cuisines of the Middle East. BELOW Red peppers drying in the sun in Nabeul, Tunisia.

FRIED AUBERGINE AND PEPPER SALAD

PREPARATION TIME
1 hour 35 minutes, including 1
    hour salting and 30 minutes
    cooking

1 medium aubergine
salt
3–4 green peppers
45 ml [3 tbsp] oil
5 ml [1 tsp] coriander seed
1 clove garlic
3 tomatoes
15 ml [1 tbsp] vinegar

TO GARNISH
15 ml [1 tbsp] chopped parsley

1 Cut the aubergine into 3 cm [1 in.] cubes. Put them in a colander, sprinkle with salt, cover with a plate and put a weight on top. Leave for about an hour.
2 Cut the peppers into pieces about 3 cm [1 in.] square, discarding the seeds. Fry them in hot oil until the skin begins to crack, then lower the heat.
3 Take out the aubergines one handful at a time and dry them by pressing between sheets of kitchen paper. Add each dried handful to the pan, stir and dry the next handful. Let the mixture cook on medium heat. If the vegetables stick to the pan, add a little water and scrape the pan thoroughly.
4 Roast the coriander seed gently in a non-stick pan, rolling it around frequently until lightly coloured. Crush it and add to the vegetables. Chop the garlic very finely, and add.
5 Skin and chop the tomatoes and add them to the pan. Cook over a medium heat for about 15 minutes, until the aubergines and tomatoes are fairly mushy, and the pieces of pepper cooked but still holding their shape.
6 Transfer the cooked vegetables to a bowl, add a little vinegar, stir gently, taste and add more vinegar or salt as required. Tip into a shallow serving bowl and serve cold, sprinkled with chopped parsley.

For a piquant flavour, cook a small fresh chilli, deseeded and chopped, with the peppers.

YOGHURT AND CUCUMBER SALAD

PREPARATION TIME
10 minutes

1 clove garlic
1 140 g [5 oz] carton
    natural yoghurt
salt to taste
1 small 'Cyprus' type
    cucumber, or ½ a European
    cucumber
5 ml [1 tsp] crushed dried mint

1 Crush the garlic into a bowl. Add the yoghurt and beat till smooth. Add salt to taste.
2 Chop the cucumber into cubes and mix into the yoghurt with the dried mint. Taste, and adjust the seasoning. Serve cool.

YOGHURT AND ONION SALAD This combination, using onion rather than cucumber, is not strictly Middle Eastern, being Indian inspired, but it makes a delicious *mezze*. Slice 1 large or 2 medium onions very thinly. Put in a bowl, sprinkle with salt and the juice of ½ lemon and leave to marinate for at least 1 hour. Add the yoghurt and beat very well. Flavour with crushed dried mint, and a pinch of cayenne pepper if you like. Serve cool.

FRENCH BEAN SALAD

PREPARATION TIME
30–40 minutes, including
    20–30 minutes cooking

15–30 ml [1–2 tbsp] olive oil
250 g [8 oz] French beans
salt to taste
juice of ½–1 lime or lemon, to
    taste

For this salad you should use very young, fresh beans which do not have strings that need removing.

1 Choose a heavy-based pan which takes the beans in one layer. Pour in just enough olive oil to thinly coat the bottom. Wash, top and tail the beans. Put them in the pan and add salt and some lime or lemon juice – you can add more later if necessary. Barely cover the beans with water. Shake the pan well and bring to the boil, then immediately lower the heat to simmer and cover the pan.
2 Shake the pan from time to time. After about 20 minutes, check if the beans are cooked. This depends on how you like your vegetables; to my taste they are ready as soon as the colour turns olive green. They will still be crunchy but will have just lost their raw taste. This takes 20 to 30 minutes. If you prefer to cook the beans longer, you may need to add a little more water.
3 Arrange the beans in an hors d'oeuvre dish. Reduce the liquid left in the pan and pour it over them. Taste, and add more salt or lime or lemon juice if needed. Serve cold.

If made in larger quantities, they make a delicious simple vegetable dish. The flavouring can be varied by the addition of thinly sliced garlic, chopped parsley or coriander.

SPINACH OR SWISS CHARD SALAD The stems of spinach or Swiss chard are also delicious cooked in this way. Discard any discoloured stems, trim the remaining stems and, in the case of Swiss chard, cut into strips. Cook as above for 10 to 15 minutes.

French Bean Salad, Fried Aubergine and Pepper Salad and Yoghurt and Cucumber Salad

SKINNING TOMATOES
This method is particularly appropriate for tomatoes used in salads. Spike each tomato on a long fork and hold it over a naked flame. The skin will crack and curl up in no time.

COURGETTE SALAD The same method and seasoning can be used for very small, young courgettes – but no larger than your thumb. It can be difficult to find courgettes this small in Britain, unless you grow them yourself.

CELERY SALAD Cut the celery into 5 cm [2 in.] sticks and cook as above, but with just enough turmeric added to the vegetables to slightly colour them and add a delicate flavour.

All these salads may be eaten hot or cold.

Left to right two bowls of Tabbouleh, made with varying proportions of burghul to greenstuff, Fattoush, and Egyptian Salad

TABBOULEH

PREPARATION TIME
30 minutes, including 15
 minutes soaking

30 ml [2 tbsp] **burghul**
1 **teacupful finely chopped
 parsley**
30 ml [2 tbsp] **finely chopped
 fresh coriander**
4 **spring onions**
1 **small cucumber**
about 15 ml [1 tbsp] **fresh mint,
 or** 5 ml [1 tsp] **crushed dried
 mint**
salt and pepper to taste
juice of 1 or 2 lemons
10 ml [2 tsp] **olive oil**

This delicious lemony salad of Lebanese origin has become popular in Britain in recent years. Burghul is readily available from Middle Eastern grocers and health food shops. It should be a predominantly green salad with white specks.

1 Soak the burghul for about 15 minutes in a bowl full of water.
2 Line a colander with muslin or a tea towel and tip the burghul into it. Lift out the cloth and squeeze hard to remove as much moisture as possible. Put the burghul in a salad bowl and add the vegetables and herbs, either chopped or cut up into very small pieces. Mix well.
3 Add salt, pepper and lemon juice to taste, and again mix well. Add half the oil, mix thoroughly, then add the rest if necessary and mix again. There is enough oil when the salad glistens. Taste, and adjust the seasoning if necessary.

This salad is sometimes made with a much larger proportion of burghul, when it looks more like a rice salad: white with green specks. If you want to make it like this, use a teacupful of burghul to the same amount of greenstuff in the above recipe.

EGYPTIAN SALAD

PREPARATION TIME
30 minutes
1 hour wait

½ cos lettuce
2–3 small 'Cyprus' cucumbers
   or 1 small, thin European
   one
2–3 spring onions or 1 small
   sweet red onion or ½ white
   onion
2 firm tomatoes
salt to taste
juice of 1 lime or lemon
about 10 ml [2 tsp] olive oil

TO GARNISH
a few sprigs parsley, chopped

Salads of this kind are made not only in Egypt but all over the Middle East, from Greece through Turkey to Lebanon and beyond. The main feature is that the ingredients are cut into very small pieces. The dressing is made with lime or lemon juice rather than vinegar, and has a strong flavour of the juice. The salad is prepared in advance to let the flavour infuse. This suits Middle Eastern lettuces, which are of the cos type, crisp but a bit tough. If you can, use small 'Cyprus' type cucumbers. Should you have to use a large European cucumber, choose the thinnest one you can find, and remove any seeds. If you are using a round onion rather than spring onions, it should be mild: best of all are the sweet red Italian type.

1 Dice the vegetables and sprinkle them with salt, then lime or lemon juice, and mix well so that the salt dissolves. Add the oil a little at a time, mix, add more and mix again. I find that there is enough oil when the salad glistens, but you might like more; it's a question of taste.
2 Taste, adjust the seasoning, and leave in a cool place for an hour. To serve, sprinkle the parsley over the salad.

The dressing can be varied by adding a pinch of ground cumin seed or a little crushed dried mint, and the salad garnished with chopped fresh coriander instead of parsley.

FATTOUSH (TUNISIAN SALAD)

PREPARATION TIME
1 hour, including 10 minutes
   cooking

2 thick slices stale wholemeal
   bread
45 ml [3 tbsp] vinegar
1 large or 2 small green peppers
2 medium tomatoes
2–3 spring onions
100 g [4 oz] halumi cheese
a few olives and capers (optional)
1 200 g [7 oz] can tuna fish
salt to taste
1 clove garlic
5 ml [1 tsp] crushed coriander
   seed and 2.5 ml [½ tsp]
   crushed caraway seed
a dot harissa chilli sauce
30 ml [2 tbsp] oil

This is a traditional Tunisian salad, a version of 'salade niçoise', whose ingredients vary according to taste and availability.

1 Cut the bread into small cubes and moisten them with 15 ml [1 tbsp] of the vinegar diluted with twice that amount of water. Grill the peppers until the skin is blistered and black. Put them in a bowl and leave it covered with a cloth for a few minutes; this will make peeling easier.
2 Peel and coarsely chop the peppers. Skin the tomatoes and cut into cubes, discarding the pulp if watery. Chop the spring onions, including the green tops. Cut the cheese into small cubes. Stone the olives.
3 Put the soaked bread in a salad bowl with the peppers, tomatoes and onions, and the tuna, cheese and olives, plus a few capers if you like. Add salt to taste.
4 Crush the garlic. Fry the crushed spices, harissa and garlic in the oil until the garlic is golden, then add the rest of the vinegar and pour the mixture over the salad.

You can also add a Preserved Lemon (see page 139), rinsed and chopped.

CABBAGE SALAD

PREPARATION TIME
10 minutes
3 hour wait

½ small white cabbage
salt
juice of ½ lemon or 10 ml [2 tsp]
   vinegar, or a mixture of the
   two
10 ml [2 tsp] olive oil, or as
   required
5 ml [1 tsp] crushed dried mint

(picture on page 26)

This cabbage salad is not of the crisp type that you sometimes find in Greek restaurants. It is very finely shredded and softened, so that it absorbs the dressing.

1 Shred the cabbage as finely as possible and put it in a colander. Sprinkle some salt over it, put a weighted plate on top and leave for at least 3 hours. A fair amount of liquid will come out and the cabbage will soften.
2 Squeeze the cabbage hard with your hands to remove as much moisture as possible. Transfer it to a bowl and add lemon juice or vinegar, or a mixture of the two. Mix thoroughly. Then add a teaspoonful of oil, mix well, add another and mix again. There should be just enough oil to make the salad glisten.
3 Taste, add more salt if necessary, and the crushed dried mint.

You can use this cabbage salad as the basis for a mixed salad by adding some or all of the ingredients from Egyptian Salad (above).

   If you don't have time to wait 3 hours for the cabbage to soften, squeeze the liquid out after about 30 minutes in the salt, and then again after another few minutes. You must squeeze and rub the cabbage hard against the colander.

THE MEZZE TABLE

The *mezze* idea is well worth adopting for the first course of a dinner party. A large selection of appetizing delicacies is waiting for the guests to pick and choose from as soon as they arrive, allowing people to come at different times without the early arrivals starving, or spoiling their appetites with peanuts or crisps.

The great advantage for the cook is that she or he can prepare most of the dishes for a *mezze* in advance. You can therefore plan a range of dishes according to how much time you have, and how much you want to spend.

Preparing a *mezze* spread is also great fun because you don't have to make a large quantity of each dish, but select a number, contrasting in texture, shape, colour and of course flavour: crisp spinach borek, stuffed vine leaves, succulent chicken wings, dips, pickles and preserves, and olives, cheese and *crudités*.

Of course, there is no need to follow a *mezze* first course with other Middle Eastern courses: you could make any familiar main course, perhaps a roast or casserole, and finish with fruit, cheese, or your favourite pudding. And I do not want to give the impression that you have to offer lots of items for a *mezze*: any one, two or three of the recipes in this chapter would be quite enough before a traditional western meal.

Above, from left to right, front row Fila Borek with Spinach Filling, Baked Borek with Cheese Filling, Chicken Wings in Garlic and Lime Sauce, Laban Cheese Balls. *Middle row* Falafel, bowls of feta cheese and olives, Grilled Chicken Livers, Fila Pastry Tarts, Poached Brains in Turmeric and Garlic Sauce. *Back row* Cabbage Salad, Hummus Dip and Spiced Carrots

BOREK
Shaping Shortcrust Pastry Borek

  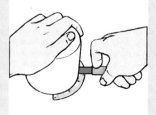 

1 Roll out the pastry into a thin circle, and put a teaspoonful of filling just off centre on it. Be careful not to let the filling spread out.

2 Fold the pastry over the filling and press all around the edge (not too close to the filling) with your thumb to seal it.

3 Trim the surplus pastry from the edge of the seam with a cup and knife or the rim of a glass.

4 Seal again by crimping all along the edge of the seam with a fork, or by pinching with your finger and thumb.

TARTS MADE FROM LEFTOVER FILA PASTRY

1 Grease an individual tart case. Arrange small rectangles of leftover fila in the centre of the case in overlapping layers.

2 Brush each rectangle lightly with melted butter as you go along. Add more overlapping layers until there are about 4 or 5 in all.

3 Spoon a good heap of filling, such as the cheese filling on page 34 mixed with another beaten egg, into the centre. Crumble the edges of the overlapping layers of fila over the filling, and any other leftover scraps, to just cover filling. Bake in a moderate oven for 20-30 minutes.

CHICKEN WINGS IN GARLIC AND LIME SAUCE

PREPARATION TIME

1 hour 25 minutes, including 1 hour marinating and 20 minutes cooking

8 chicken wings
1 clove garlic
salt to taste
juice of 1–2 limes or lemons

(picture on page 27)

When we arrived in London in 1948, postwar rationing was still in force. My family used to buy enormous bags of chicken wings every week from a famous Indian restaurateur who owned a chicken farm; until we came along, all his chicken wings had been thrown away. You might think we soon got tired of them; but we never did, for my mother cooked them in all kinds of ways, using them for almost any meat or poultry dish. And to this day I never fail to order the 'mezze' of chicken wings with lime and garlic served in the Lebanese restaurants that have sprouted up all over London. You can substitute lemon juice if limes are not available.

1 Wash the wings, cut them in halves, and put them in a bowl. Chop or slice the garlic finely and sprinkle over the wings, followed by salt and plenty of lime or lemon juice. Leave them to marinate for at least 1 hour, turning from time to time.
2 Put the wings and their marinade in a heavy-based saucepan broad enough for them to fit snugly together in a single layer. Barely cover them with water and bring to the boil. Lower the heat immediately and cover the pan. Simmer for about 15 minutes. Shake the pan from time to time to prevent sticking. If they do stick, add a little water and scrape the pan. When the dish is ready, the juices should have reduced to a thick sauce. Serve the wings hot on a small *mezze* plate with the pan juices poured over them.

This way of cooking chicken is very similar to the Philippino dish Adobo which has a different marinade: soy sauce is used instead of salt and vinegar replaces the lemon juice.

GRILLED CHICKEN LIVERS

PREPARATION TIME

7 minutes, including 2 minutes cooking

8 chicken livers
oil for grill pan (optional)
salt and pepper to taste

(picture on page 26)

1 Rinse and dry the livers, and separate each into its two lobes.
2 Heat the grill to high or, if using a cast-iron grill pan on top of the stove, get it very hot, then oil it lightly with a brush or a piece of cotton wool. Grill the livers on both sides as quickly as possible to avoid drying them out. Take care not to overcook them: each side will take about 1 minute. Sprinkle with salt (sea salt is particularly good) and pepper, and serve.

The livers may also be sautéed in hot butter, seasoned and served with a squeeze of lemon juice.

POACHED BRAINS IN TURMERIC AND GARLIC SAUCE

PREPARATION TIME
30 minutes soaking
30 minutes, including 20 minutes cooking

2 sets calf's brains
15 ml [1 tbsp] vinegar
15–30 ml [1–2 tbsp] oil
juice of 1 lemon, or more to taste
1 clove garlic
5 ml [1 tsp] turmeric
salt and pepper to taste

TO GARNISH
a few sprigs parsley, chopped

(picture on page 27)

1 Wash the brains in cold running water. Soak them in cold water and vinegar for about 30 minutes. Rinse and remove the membrane. (With frozen brains, the membrane disappears anyway.)

2 Choose a pan into which the brains will fit in one layer. Put in just enough oil to coat the bottom, and the juice of a lemon. Slice and add the garlic. Lay the brains carefully in the pan and barely cover them with water. Add the turmeric and salt and pepper to taste, and swirl the pan to spread the liquid over the brains. Bring to the boil, then reduce the heat to a gentle simmer and cover the pan. Check after a few minutes that the liquid is not drying up, and add more water if necessary. The brains are ready as soon as they are firm, after about 20 minutes. Be careful not to overcook them.

3 Put the brains on a plate to cool, and reduce the liquid in the pan if necessary; it should be fairly thick. Cut the brains into slices with a sharp knife. Arrange them on an hors d'oeuvre dish and pour the liquid over them. Add more lemon juice and chopped parsley if you like. Serve cold.

FRIED BRAINS Prepare the brains as above, then poach in salted water with a little vinegar. Allow them to cool, then cut into slices. Put a beaten egg yolk on a small plate, and some flour or very fine dried breadcrumbs on another. Coat each slice in the egg, then the flour. Fry gently in hot oil or clarified butter for a few minutes. Serve hot with wedges of lemon.

BELOW A market stall at Djerba, on a small island off the Tunisian coast, selling cinnamon bark, powdered green henna, lime blossom tea and other cooking and medicinal herbs.

LAHME BI AJEEN (LEBANESE MEAT TARTLETS)

PREPARATION TIME
30 minutes, including 15
minutes cooking

MAKES ABOUT 20 TARTLETS

BASE
bread dough made with 250 g
[8 oz] flour

FILLING
120 g [4 oz] minced lamb or
beef, or a mixture of the two
1 medium onion
salt and pepper to taste
5 ml [1 tsp] ground allspice
15 ml [1 tbsp] finely chopped
parsley
juice of ½ lemon, or to taste
30 g [1 oz] pine nuts

TO BAKE
a handful bran

These are like miniature meat pizzas. Use the dough on page 134 or your favourite bread dough.

1 When you have prepared the dough, make the filling. Put the meat into a mixing bowl and grate the onion straight into it. Add salt, pepper, allspice, parsley and lemon juice. Taste, and adjust the seasoning.
2 Preheat the oven to 230°C [450°F, gas 8]. Quickly fry the pine nuts in a dry pan until slightly brown, and add to the mixture.
3 Knead the dough very well (see page 134). Oil your hands lightly, take a walnut-sized piece of dough and knead it well. Roll it or flatten it with your hand into a circle no thicker than a 10p piece, about 2 mm [$\frac{1}{10}$ in.]. Draw your thumbs across the dough from the centre to the edges to make a slightly raised rim to hold the filling.
4 Make all the bases and put a pile of filling in the middle of each. Sprinkle a dry baking sheet with bran and set the tartlets on it in rows. Bake for about 15 minutes, until the meat is done and the bread bases are cooked but still soft.

The filling may be flavoured with a small amount of crushed dried limes (see page 10) or a sprinkling of sumac instead of lemon juice.

MEATLESS TARTLETS Mix one of the herb or spice mixtures on page 140 with a little olive oil and spread on the bases instead of the meat mixture above. A sprinkling of sesame seeds gives a nice crunchy texture.

BRIK A L'OEUF

PREPARATION TIME
30 minutes, including 5–10
minutes cooking

MAKES 4 BRIK

1 200 g [7 oz] can tuna
8 small sheets Chinese spring
roll, fila or strudel pastry
15 ml [1 tbsp] oil + oil for deep
frying
4 eggs
120 g [4 oz] grated cheese
capers
salt and pepper to taste

Brik, the most famous of Tunisian snacks, are a special, large kind of deep-fried borek. In fact the word brik is simply the North African pronunciation of the original Turkish 'börek'. They may contain an infinite variety of fillings, the most spectacular of which is a whole egg (Brik à l'Oeuf, below). Fillings may also be made of any suitable leftovers.

The wafer-thin pastry, called 'malsouqa', comes in circles. It is sold in Tunisia and France. Chinese spring roll pastry is a good substitute; fila and strudel pastry are also satisfactory.

Brik are tricky to make at first, but once you have acquired the skill they make a quick and very delicious snack. It is vital to have the filling ready first. The skill lies in the speed with which you fold the pastry into a packet and slip it into the hot oil. If you are a beginner, it is probably a good idea to practise with the variation below.

1 Crumble the tuna. Cut the pastry into 12 cm [5 in.] squares and use two thicknesses of pastry for each brik. Put one of the squares on a plate, brush it lightly with oil and put the other square on top of it.
2 Put a large tablespoonful of tuna on to the square of pastry, to one side of the centre. Make a hollow in the mound of tuna and break an egg into the hollow. Sprinkle grated cheese and capers on top, and add salt and pepper to taste. Fold the pastry over the filling to make a rectangular packet, or a triangular one, whichever is easier. Moisten the seams with water to seal.
3 Heat the oil. Test the temperature by adding a small piece of pastry: when it sizzles to the surface, the oil is ready.
4 Slide the brik carefully into the oil and fry until golden brown, basting and turning once if it is not completely submerged in oil. It cooks almost immediately. Drain on kitchen paper.

Eating this brik also requires practice. The idea is to suck out the runny egg, at the same time getting a mouthful of tuna and crisp pastry.

FISH AND POTATO BRIK No less delicious, but easier to make and eat! The filling may be made with leftovers from the fish stew on page 53, or some similar dish. Mash together a piece of cooked fish and a cooked potato. Add 15 ml [1 tbsp] of chopped parsley, 2.5 ml [½ tsp] of turmeric and a spot of harissa or other hot red chilli sauce. Beat an egg into the mixture. There should be enough filling for several briks.

OPPOSITE Brik à l'Oeuf, rectangular or triangular pastry packets (*top left*), Lahme bi Ajeen (*bottom left*), Baked Borek with Khandrajo Filling (*right*) and Fried Borek with Meat Filling (*centre right*)

BOREK

In Turkish 'borek' means, roughly, a pasty. The Arabic word is 'faytir'. There are many kinds, small and large, savoury and sweet. Small savoury borek are highly popular as *mezze*. The smaller and more delicate you can make them, the better they are. Fillings are endlessly varied: four are given below, and the other fillings elsewhere in this book should give you plenty of ideas for creating your own. Let your imagination be your guide. Borek may be made with shortcrust, flaky or ready-made fila pastry. There are almost as many variations for pastry as there are for fillings, and each cook uses her own favourite. My own favourite recipe for pastry is given below. It was given to my mother by Victoria Cohen, a neighbour in Cairo. Not only is it very good, it is also extremely easy to make, though it defies all conventional notions of pastry making. The quantities in the recipe are governed by volume. The French principal of one cookery school was really shocked the first time she saw me making it, but she was so impressed by the result that now she insists that I include it in all my demonstrations. You can use this pastry for quiches, savoury tarts and so on, as well as for borek. At that particular school they use it, made with sugar instead of salt, for their Christmas mince pies.

BAKED BOREK WITH KHANDRAJO FILLING

PREPARATION TIME
1 hour 25 minutes, including 1
    hour 10 minutes cooking

MAKES 20 BOREK

FILLING
1 large onion
15–30 ml [1–2 tbsp] oil
2 large aubergines
salt and pepper to taste
6–7 tomatoes, or a 400 g [14
    oz] can peeled tomatoes

PASTRY
50 g [2 oz] butter
same volume oil and water (see
    right)
5 ml [1 tsp] salt
250 g [about 8 oz] flour

TO GLAZE
milk or egg yolk

(picture on page 31)

The Khandrajo filling is one my grandmother used to make. It is an aubergine, onion and tomato mixture rather like 'ratatouille'. Make the filling first so that it has time to cool.

Filling

1 Cut the onion into small chunks and put it in a heavy-based pan with a thin layer of oil. Cook over a medium to low heat to soften it. Meanwhile, wash and dry the aubergines and, without peeling, cut into 3 cm [1 in.] cubes. When the onion begins to colour, mix in the aubergine, salt and pepper.

2 If you are using fresh tomatoes, peel them and remove any watery bits; if you are using canned tomatoes, drain and reserve the liquid. When the mixture gets a little darker, add the tomatoes and stir very thoroughly. Continue cooking on medium heat, stirring from time to time.

3 After about 20 minutes increase the heat and stir constantly until the mixture becomes fairly dry and on the dark side. If it sticks to the pan, add a little water or canned tomato liquid and scrape well. When the mixture is really quite dry, transfer it to a bowl and leave to cool. It must be absolutely cold before you can use it. If any oil rises to the surface, spoon it off or soak it up with kitchen paper.

Short pastry

4 Cut up the butter and melt it very gently over a low heat, taking care not to cook it. Pour it into a small cup standing on a flat surface. Then pour it into a large mixing bowl. The butter will have left a mark inside the cup; this is the measuring mark.

5 Fill the cup with oil up to the same mark and pour this into the bowl. Measure an equal quantity of water in the same way. Add with the salt to the bowl and stir.

6 Using a large wooden spoon, add one spoonful of flour at a time, stirring constantly to mix it in. It looks rather unpleasant, like a sauce full of lumps, at first; but don't worry. Just go on adding and mixing, and the mixture will start to look more like dough, then pastry. The proportions are about right when the pastry comes away from the sides of the bowl, leaving it clean. By then it will have taken up very roughly 250 g [8 oz] of flour. Gather the pastry into the centre of the bowl with your hands, and transfer it to a work surface. If the pastry is too soft, and needs more flour, put some in a pile on one side. Roll the ball of pastry in the flour so that it takes up a little at a time. Then, with a quick, firm twist of your hand, incorporate the flour. French cooks call this *fraiser*.

7 The pastry is now ready to use; unlike other pastries it does not need a resting period.
* However, it can be prepared in advance to this stage, wrapped in foil and stored in the refrigerator. It is easier to handle after refrigeration.

8 Just before you start filling the borek, preheat the oven to 190°C [375°F, gas 5]. To make small borek, take a piece of pastry about the size of an egg. Press it into a flat disc in your hand, ensuring that there are no cracks in it. Then flatten it more on a board and roll it into a thin circle.

SOME BOREK SHAPES

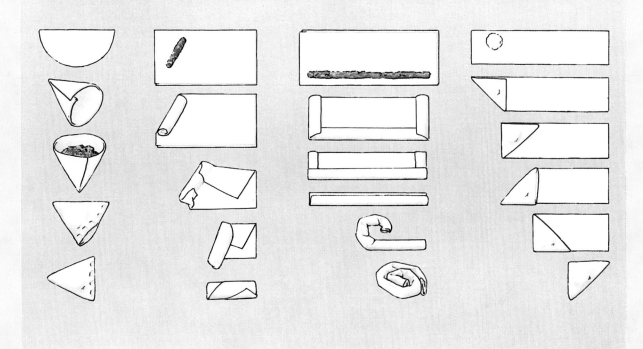

Pastry for Frying
CONES

1 Cut a circle of pastry 12cm (5 in.) in diameter in half and moisten the straight edge.

2 Form the semicircle into a cone by folding the straight edge in half and sealing it.

3 Open out the cone and put in about half a teaspoonful of filling.

4 Close the top with wet fingers.

5 Crimp the seams with your finger and thumb.

With Fila Pastry
CIGAR SHAPES

1 Put a sausage-shaped roll of filling diagonally across one corner of a double layer of fila, about 22cm (9 in.) by 12cm (5 in.).

2 Starting from the same corner, roll the pastry diagonally, folding in the sides as you go along to make a small, neat, cigar-shaped parcel.

With Fila Pastry
COILS

1 Spread a narrow line of filling along one edge of a double layer of fila, about 30cm (12 in.) by 12cm (5 in.), leaving a small border of pastry uncovered at each end.

2 Fold in the two short edges and one long edge to enclose the filling.

3 Starting at the filling edge, roll the pastry into a long thin sausage shape.

4 & 5 Form a tight coil by holding one end of the pastry and twisting the rest of the roll around it.

All Pastries
TRIANGLES

1 Put a teaspoonful of filling in a small heap on a double layer of fila about 30cm (12 in.) by 7cm (3 in.).

2 Fold into a triangle as shown, making sure that the filling remains completely enclosed in the pastry.

9 Put about 5 ml [1 tsp] of the filling just off centre on the pastry. Be very careful to drop it in a neat pile. If it spreads out over the pastry you will not be able to seal the borek. Fold the pastry over to make a semicircle, and press all around with your thumb to seal it. Don't press too close to the filling. There must be a space around it to let it expand during cooking. Trim the edge of the seam with the rim of a glass, or a pastry cutter. Add the trimmings to the main lump of dough. Make sure of a good seal by crimping all along the seam with a fork, or by pinching with your finger and thumb.

10 Brush the borek with milk or beaten egg yolk and put them on a baking sheet. With this pastry, you do not need to grease or flour it. Bake for 30 to 40 minutes. Check that they are done by lifting one up. The underneath should be just beginning to colour. Transfer to a cooling rack and serve warm or cold.

CHEESE FILLING FOR BOREK

PREPARATION TIME
10 minutes

MAKES ENOUGH FOR 20 BOREK

230 g [8 oz] grated cheese (see right)
breadcrumbs (if necessary)
1 size 2 [large] egg
5 ml [1 tsp] crushed dried mint (optional)

Cheese is one of the traditional fillings for all kinds of borek, baked or fried. The flavour must be well balanced: mild cheeses are too bland when cooked, strong ones too overpowering, so it is usual to mix them. A very strong mixture can be toned down by adding a small amount of fresh breadcrumbs. A few experiments will help you to achieve a good flavour with whatever cheese you have available. You might begin by trying the following combinations: 3 parts mild Cheddar to 1 part feta; or 3 parts strong matured Cheddar to 1 part feta plus a handful of fresh breadcrumbs; or one of the mild cheeses with just 15 g [$\frac{1}{2}$ oz] of very strong blue cheese; or 6 parts mild cheese to 1 part each of Parmesan and demi-sel or curd cheese. Combine the grated cheese with the egg. The consistency should be softish, but firmer than dropping consistency. Adjust it with more cheese or breadcrumbs. Add mint if you like.

FRIED BOREK WITH MEAT FILLING

PREPARATION TIME
1 hour 10 minutes, including 30 minutes wait and 25 minutes cooking

MAKES 30 BOREK

FILLING
1 medium onion
about 15 ml [1 tbsp] oil
1 clove garlic
120 g [4 oz] minced lamb or beef, or a mixture of the two
5 ml [1 tsp] ground allspice
1.5 ml [$\frac{1}{4}$ tsp] grated nutmeg
salt and pepper to taste
1 egg
15–30 ml [1–2 tbsp] chopped parsley

PASTRY
225 g [8 oz] flour
5 ml [1 tsp] salt
30 ml [2 tbsp] oil
75 ml [5 tbsp] lukewarm water

oil for deep frying

(picture on page 31)

Make the filling first so that it has time to cool before you use it. My favourite pastry, on page 32, is too rich for frying. The one given here is more suitable.

Filling

1 Grate or chop the onion very finely, put in a saucepan with a little oil, and cook over a medium heat for 10 to 15 minutes, or until soft and transparent.

2 Chop the garlic very finely and add to the onion. Increase the heat and cook, stirring, till the onion turns golden brown. Add the meat, squashing it against the side of the pan. If it sticks to the bottom, scrape well. Keep stirring till the meat begins to brown. Add the pepper and allspice, a little nutmeg, and salt. Mix well and keep stirring until the meat is nicely brown. If it sticks, scrape the pan thoroughly and add a little water.

3 Transfer the mixture to a bowl. Beat the egg and mix it in to soften the mixture. Stir in parsley to taste. Let the mixture cool completely before using it.

Pastry for frying

4 Sift the flour and salt into a bowl. Make a hole in the centre. Pour the oil and water into the hole and mix with two knives until all the flour is combined. If you are using a food processor, add only the oil at first, and pour in water a little at a time as you may not need it all. Gather the pastry with your hands and knead very well until it is even and soft. This takes a good 10 minutes. Form the dough into a smooth ball, cover the bowl with a damp cloth and leave to rest for about 30 minutes in the refrigerator.

5 Put a little oil on your hands and rub it into the rolling pin. Take a lump of dough the size of a walnut. Knead it very thoroughly until it is perfectly smooth, and form it into a round ball without creases. Roll the pastry out into a circle, as thinly as you can; it must be really transparent. Put a saucer about 12 cm [5 in.] in diameter on the circle and trim around it. Save the trimmings and use later. Cut the circle in half with a sharp knife. You may prefer to roll out all the pastry circles before shaping and filling. If so, brush one side of each circle with a little oil, then stack them.

6 Follow the step-by-step instructions on page 33. Wet your finger and run it along the straight edge. Fold the pastry in two and close to form a cone shape. Open out the cone, hold it upright and put in about half a teaspoonful of filling. Close the top with wet fingers. Crimp the seams at intervals with your thumb and forefinger to make a frilly edge.

* This pastry can be prepared in advance, and is actually improved by freezing, which lightens the texture. You can freeze the uncooked borek first loose on a tray, then packed in bags, and fry them straight from the freezer.

7 Deep fry for less than a minute, until puffed up and golden, then put on kitchen paper to absorb the oil. Serve hot.

Traditional additions to the filling are some chopped cooked spinach with a squeeze of lemon juice; or a hard-boiled egg cut up into very small pieces (not chopped); or a handful of pine nuts quickly browned in a dry frying pan.

> TESTING OIL TEMPERATURE
>
> Cut off a small piece of whatever you are going to fry, or take a pinch of breadcrumbs if you are using them, and drop into the oil. When the food sizzles to the surface, the oil is hot enough. For safety, I use a long-handled spoon to slowly ease the food into the oil.

Baked Borek with Cheese Filling and Fila Pastry Borek with Spinach Filling

FILA PASTRY BOREK WITH SPINACH FILLING

The traditional coil shape can be achieved only if using very fresh and pliable fila pastry (see the advice on handling fila pastry on page 130).

PREPARATION TIME
1 hour 15 minutes, including 30 minutes cooking

MAKES 16–18 BOREK

1 kg [2 lb] **fresh spinach or 500 g [1 lb] frozen leaf spinach**
salt to taste
300 g [10 oz] **grated Cheddar cheese**
60 g [2 oz] **curd or demi-sel cheese**
2 size 2 [large] **eggs**
juice of 1 lemon, or to taste
pepper and grated nutmeg to taste
450 g [1 lb] **fila pastry**
oil or melted butter

1 If you are using fresh spinach, wash it well, tear it up and put in a saucepan. Sprinkle it with salt, cover the pan and cook on a low heat, turning frequently, for a few minutes. Turn the pan on its side and squeeze the spinach to remove as much moisture as possible, then turn up the heat to dry it more. Tip it into a sieve and press out the last of the water. If using frozen spinach, thaw it in a pan with salt, then dry it out as above. It is important that the salt is added in the first stages of cooking; if added later, there is a risk that it will draw more moisture out of the spinach.

2 Chop the spinach roughly and put it in a bowl with the cheese, eggs and lemon juice. Stir well; the mixture should be quite firm. Taste, and add more salt, pepper and a little nutmeg.

3 Cut the fila sheets into rectangles about 30 cm [12 in.] by 12 cm [5 in.]. Roll up the cut sheets together and keep them covered with one or two damp cloths. Put a bowl at each end of the rolled up sheets, and hang the cloths over them so that they do not touch the pastry. Remove one sheet at a time as it is needed.

4 Preheat the oven to 190°C [375°F, gas 5]. Brush one side of the fila sheet lightly all over with oil or melted butter. Place another fila sheet on top of it. Take about a tablespoon of filling and spread it in a line as thick as your little finger all along one long edge of the rectangle. (Follow the step-by-step instructions on page 33.) Leave about 1 cm [$\frac{3}{8}$ in.] at each end of the pastry free of filling. Roll the pastry lengthways into a thin sausage then form into a coil. Put it on an oiled baking sheet and brush the top and sides with oil. The borek should be packed tightly together on the sheet to keep them from uncoiling when baked.

5 Bake in the oven for about 30 minutes. Check after about 25 minutes to see if they are done. They should be golden brown on top.

SOUPS

In the Middle East, like anywhere else, soups are enjoyed in every home. But I confess to being embarrassed to write this for, until I came to England in my twenties and started cooking, I never ate any soups. Now they are among the things I most enjoy making and eating, as they give such great creative scope. All kinds of pulses, fresh vegetables, meats, poultry or fish and scraps or bones of these, with herbs and spices available in Britain, can be turned into exciting soups with a Middle Eastern flavour.

There is often very little difference between a soup and a stew; the quantity of water is what distinguishes one from the other. I have grouped the soup recipes into a few general categories. First come the soups based on meat, chicken or fish broths and stocks. For these I have given a simple recipe for a basic stock that is well worth making for storage as a reserve. Second are meat and vegetable soups. Third are those based on purées of pulses. The fourth category comprises what I would call special soups: Melokheya from Egypt and Trahanas from Cyprus. The former is an old favourite of mine: in fact it was the only soup I ever ate in my youth. The second is a recent discovery that I have adopted with enthusiasm.

Two rich vegetable soups and two stock-based soups (*clockwise from the top*) Shorba and Rich Meatless Soup, Yoghurt Soup with Chicken Rissoles and Parsley, and Egg and Lemon Soup with Meat Balls

37

STOCK AND BROTH

I usually make stock with whatever is available: bones and any meat or poultry, or fish bones, heads and trimmings, and with a couple of carrots, a leek, an onion, some parsley stalks (which have more flavour than the leaves), and salt and pepper. I never include any extra flavouring when making basic stock in advance, since I intend to use it for different soups or other dishes, each of which will have its own flavouring.

I find it better not to add the vegetables to the pot at the beginning, but after the water boils and all the scum has been skimmed off. Floating vegetables makes this difficult. After adding the vegetables, whole or cut into chunks, I bring the water back to the boil slowly, add salt and pepper, and simmer very gently with the lid set on the pan at a tilt to let out some of the steam. If I am making a broth to be used immediately, I continue cooking it until it no longer tastes watery. When making meat or poultry stock in advance, however, it is better to continue cooking until the liquid is reduced to about half its original volume, making a really strong stock which is a fine basis for soups and other dishes. This is diluted when needed to make broth.

When the stock is ready, I strain it through a sieve into a bowl and leave it to cool. Then I leave it in the refrigerator overnight. The fat rises to the surface and congeals into a solid mass which is easy to remove. After this, I warm the stock and strain it again through a sieve lined with kitchen paper into a saucepan. This is has to be done gently so that the sediment stays at the bottom of the bowl. Then I bring it to the boil for a couple of minutes and leave it to cool. The result is a pure, strong stock, well worth all the trouble.

When making a poultry broth with an entire bird rather than just the carcase or trimmings, I save the meat as soon as it is cooked, cutting it off the carcase and returning the carcase to the pot. The meat can either be used for another dish or added to the stock at a later stage. This is because the meat of factory-farmed chickens cooks long before any flavour is imparted to the broth. Of course, if you use a boiling fowl, or a corn-fed bird, this does not apply.

For making a fish broth, the bones and heads of white fish are ideal. The fish should not be simmered for more than 20 to 30 minutes. To reduce it to keep for later use, I strain the stock and continue simmering without the solids.

Although I do not like bought stock cubes as the only basis of a soup, they are useful for adding to a dish that needs to be enriched, or used to stretch a soup if unexpected guests arrive.

A wide range of spices and grains on sale from sacks in the souk at Fez. Many spices are sold whole, then mixed, roasted and ground for use in a particular dish. Those shown here include root ginger, red peppers, cloves and allspice berries. The grains include couscous and various sizes of burghul, or cracked wheat.

EGG AND LEMON SOUP WITH MEAT BALLS

PREPARATION TIME
1 hour 15 minutes, including
   45 minutes cooking

about 1 litre [1¾ pints] meat or
   chicken stock
about 500 ml [1 pint] water
3–4 sticks celery
4 small potatoes, or 1–2 larger
   ones
120 g [4 oz] lean veal, lamb,
   beef or chicken
1 small onion
2 cloves garlic
45 ml [3 tbsp] chopped parsley
salt and pepper to taste
a pinch ground allspice
juice of 1–2 lemons
2 eggs

TO GARNISH
a few sprigs parsley, chopped

TO SERVE
lemon wedges

(picture on page 37)

The combination of egg and lemon with a rich broth to give a distinctive, tangy flavour is a favourite one all over the Middle East, both for soups and for sauces. In Arabic it is known as 'beid bi lamoun', in Greek 'avgolemono'; both simply mean 'egg and lemon'. The broth may be made from a chicken, veal or fish stock; the soup may include rice, vermicelli (or other small pasta), pieces of meat, chicken or fish, minced meat or chicken balls or fish rissoles, and vegetables, usually celery and potatoes. Here is one recipe from the immense variety: do not hesitate to try changes to suit your own taste.

1 If you are using stock which has been prepared in advance, dilute it with about 500 ml [1 pint] water to the amount required and bring to a gentle boil. (If using freshly made broth, simply bring it to simmering point.) Trim and wash the celery, saving some leaves if you want to add them to the meat balls instead of parsley. Cut it into 6 cm [2½ in.] lengths, removing any tough strings, and add it to the broth. Wash the potatoes, peel them if you like, cut them into chunks if they are large, and add to the broth.

2 Prepare the meat balls. Mince the meat and put it in a mixing bowl. Grate in the onion and garlic. Add chopped parsley or celery leaves, salt, pepper and allspice. Knead the mixture thoroughly, then taste and adjust the seasoning. Damp your hands slightly and form the mixture into walnut-sized balls, kneading each well until quite smooth. Keep your hands just damp and they will not stick (see page 77).

3 When the vegetables are cooked, gently slide the meat balls into the soup and continue simmering gently for about another 15 minutes.

4 Meanwhile, beat the juice of 1 to 2 lemons, according to taste, with the eggs in a bowl. Add a ladleful of the hot broth and continue beating, then add several more ladlefuls, beating all the time.

5 Remove the meat balls and vegetables carefully from the soup with a slotted spoon. Put them in a soup tureen and keep warm. Remove the pan from the heat and pour the egg and lemon mixture gradually into the soup, beating all the time. Return the pan to a low heat to thicken the soup gently, taking care not to let it boil or it may curdle. Pour it into the tureen and garnish with a little chopped parsley. Serve with wedges of lemon, for those who like the lemon flavour even more pronounced.

You can vary the seasoning of the meat balls with any herb or spice that appeals to you, or use a fish broth as the basis of the soup and make some fish balls (see page 52).

YOGHURT SOUP WITH CHICKEN RISSOLES AND PARSLEY

PREPARATION TIME
1 hour 15 minutes, including
   45 minutes cooking

1.2 litres [2 pints] chicken or
   veal broth
120 g [4 oz] cooked chicken
1 medium onion
30 g [1 oz] cooked long grain
   rice
1 egg + 1 extra yolk
5 ml [1 tsp] crushed dried mint
salt and pepper to taste
75 ml [5 tbsp] very finely
   chopped parsley
300 ml [½ pint] natural yoghurt

(picture on page 37)

Another way of giving a tangy flavour to a soup is to use yoghurt rather than lemon juice. Be careful that the yoghurt does not separate.

1 Pour the broth into a large, heavy-based pan with a lid. Cover, and bring it to a gentle boil.

2 Meanwhile, make the chicken rissoles. Mince the cooked chicken, grate the onion and mix both with the rice. Knead very well to blend evenly. Beat an egg and add a little at a time to bind the mixture. It should not be sloppy; if it is, add some fresh breadcrumbs. Mix in a teaspoonful of dried mint, and salt and pepper.

3 Scatter the parsley all over a tray. Form the chicken mixture into walnut-sized rissoles and gently roll them in the parsley until they are completely covered.

* The dish can be prepared in advance to this stage.

4 About 15 minutes before serving, carefully lower the rissoles into the broth, which should be simmering. Keep it simmering for the rest of the cooking time. Some of the parsley will come off, but you will be surprised how much will stick to the rissoles if it has been chopped very finely.

5 Carefully transfer the rissoles to a soup tureen and keep warm. Beat the yoghurt and egg yolk in a bowl and add some hot broth, a tablespoonful at a time, stirring constantly. (This will prevent the yoghurt from separating, provided that it is not allowed to boil.) Add the yoghurt to the broth, heat gently to serving temperature and pour over the rissoles.

RICH MEATLESS SOUP

PREPARATION TIME
55 minutes, including 45
    minutes cooking

1 fresh or dried chilli
1 medium onion
5 cloves garlic
5 ml [1 tsp] crushed caraway
    seed
4 tomatoes, or a 200 g [7 oz]
    can
15 ml [1 tbsp] oil
45 ml [3 tbsp] chopped fresh
    coriander
salt and pepper to taste
about 120 g [4 oz] coarse
    semolina or long grain rice

TO GARNISH
a few sprigs fresh mint,
    chopped

(picture on page 37)

This is sometimes called 'poor man's soup' because it is meatless. I've renamed it for its rich flavour.

1 If using a dried chilli, soak it for a few minutes until soft. Chop the onion finely, and crush the garlic. Remove the seeds from the chilli, chop it finely, and mix well with the garlic, onion and crushed caraway seed. A food processor will do the whole job in one go, but remember to remove the chilli seeds first.

2 If using canned tomatoes, drain them and reserve the liquid; if using fresh ones, chop roughly. Fry the onion and spice mixture gently in the oil in a heavy-based saucepan. When the onion is transparent, add the tomatoes, a little of the chopped fresh coriander, salt and pepper to taste. Simmer for about 30 minutes.

3 Add enough water to make a soup consistency, bring to the boil, then turn down the heat again to simmer until the watery taste completely disappears. Add the semolina or rice and simmer for another 10 or 15 minutes until it is cooked. Taste, and adjust the seasoning. Serve garnished with the rest of the coriander and a little chopped fresh mint.

The rice or semolina can be replaced by a handful of presoaked, precooked dried chickpeas or haricot beans, added at step 3.

SHORBA

PREPARATION TIME
8 hours soaking
1 hour 5 minutes, including 50
    minutes cooking

50 g [2 oz] chickpeas
30 ml [2 tbsp] oil
2 medium onions
450 g [1 lb] stewing lamb
5–6 medium tomatoes or
    1 400 g [14 oz] can
125 g [4 oz] French beans
2 medium potatoes
125 g [4 oz] broad beans, fresh
    or frozen
4–5 sprigs each fresh mint and
    fresh coriander
salt and pepper to taste
5 ml [1 tsp] paprika
30 ml [2 tbsp] tomato purée
a teacupful water
1 medium courgette
1 medium green pepper
100 g [3½ oz] vermicelli

(picture on page 37)

'Shorba' is the Arabic word for soup. However, the Algerian friend who cooked it for me insists that this is its name since other soups, such as fava bean soup and meat ball and rice soup, are defined by their main ingredients.

1 Cover the chickpeas with water in a bowl and leave to soak for at least 8 hours.

2 Pour enough oil into a heavy-based saucepan to line the bottom and set it over a medium heat. Roughly chop the onions and add them to the pan. Cut the meat into cubes and add. Stir thoroughly after every addition. Leave to cook over a medium heat, stirring from time to time.

3 As you prepare the vegetables, add them to the pan. If using fresh tomatoes, skin and chop them; drain and chop canned ones, reserving the liquid. Top and tail the French beans, removing any strings, and halve them. Wash and scrape the potatoes (or I prefer to keep the skin on) and, if they are large, cut into chunks. If using fresh broad beans, pod them; frozen ones may be added straight from the freezer. Peel the chickpeas if necessary. Remove and reserve the leaves of the mint and coriander, tie the stalks into a bundle and add to the pan.

4 Add the chickpeas, pepper and paprika to taste after all the vegetables, and the tomato purée diluted in a teacupful of water or the juice from the can of tomatoes. Bring to the boil, then lower to simmering point and cook, half covered, for 1 hour or until the chickpeas are tender. Add salt to taste.

5 Slightly scrape the courgette, deseed the pepper and cut both into large chunks. Add to the soup with enough water to cover the vegetables by 5 cm [2 in.]. Bring to the boil. Taste, and adjust the seasoning. Lower the heat and simmer, half covered, for another 20 minutes or so. Taste again and, if the soup still tastes watery, increase the heat and reduce further.

* The soup may be prepared in advance to this stage.

6 Chop the mint and coriander leaves. Crush the vermicelli into the soup and cook for another 5 minutes or until it is tender. Remove the bundle of herbs, add the chopped mint and coriander and serve.

Beef can be substituted for the lamb (shin of beef gives a delicious flavour to the soup, but of course requires a longer time to cook), or a boiler chicken will give yet another stock. Fresh peas and carrots can also be added. The distinctive flavour is that produced by the particular way of using the herb first in sprigs during the cooking, then adding the chopped leaves just before serving.

Clockwise from the top Lentil Soup, Trahanas Soup, Haricot Bean Soup and Melokheya, a classic Egyptian dish

LENTIL SOUP

PREPARATION TIME
1 hour 15 minutes, including 1
    hour cooking

180 g [6 oz] **red lentils**
about 15 ml [1 tbsp] **oil or
    clarified butter**
1 medium **onion**
salt and pepper to taste

TA'LEYA
2–3 cloves **garlic**
5 ml [1 tsp] **oil or clarified
    butter**
5 ml [1 tsp] **ground cumin seed**

This is another splendid soup for vegetarians. Others can use a chicken or meat stock or, as I often do, add a smoked ham bone at the beginning.

1 Spread the lentils out on a large plate and pick out any stones. Wash in several changes of water.

2 Add just enough oil or clarified butter to a large saucepan to coat the base, and set over a medium heat. Chop the onion very finely, add it to the pan and cook until soft and transparent. Then raise the heat and stir until the onion browns. Add the lentils and enough water to cover them by 3 cm [1 in.], bring to the boil and lower the heat to simmer. Half cover the pan and cook for about 30 minutes, or until the lentils are very tender.

3 Remove the lentils, leaving any remaining liquid in the pan. Purée them and return to the pan, adding more water if necessary to make a good creamy soup consistency.

4 Prepare the Ta'leya. Chop the garlic very finely. Heat a teaspoonful of oil or butter in a small pan and add the garlic. Stir; as soon as it colours, add the ground cumin seed, taking care not to burn it. Stir quickly and tip into the soup.

5 Add salt and pepper to taste, and simmer the soup for another 15 to 20 minutes.

MELOKHEYA

PREPARATION TIME
3 hours, including $2\frac{1}{2}$ hours cooking

about 120 g [4 oz] **dried melokheya**

BROTH
1–2 **marrow bones**
750 g [$1\frac{1}{2}$ lb] **shin of beef**
1 **medium onion**
2 **carrots**
1 **leek**
salt and pepper to taste
6 **cracked cardamom pods**
2.5 ml [$\frac{1}{2}$ tsp] **crushed mastic**
2 litres [$3\frac{1}{2}$ pints] **water**

TA'LEYA
4–5 **cloves garlic**
15 ml [1 tbsp] **crushed coriander seed**
10 ml [2 tsp] **clarified butter**

TO SERVE
lemon juice to taste (optional)

(picture on page 41)

This universally popular soup is a classic Egyptian dish. It is made from the leaves of a species of mallow plant, known as 'melokheya'. The dried leaves can be found quite easily in Middle Eastern food shops – the spelling of the name on the packet varies widely. Fresh bunches of 'melokheya' are also sometimes available in summer; the leaves look a bit like mint. The soup is usually made with a base of chicken stock to which you add some marrow bones. On feast days in Egypt, this is replaced by a goose, which makes it extra special. I like to use shin of beef, which gives a very rich stock.

The way in which Melokheya is served and eaten varies greatly. Each family, and indeed each individual, have their own set ritual. I like to eat Melokheya first as a soup – on its own or maybe with a small piece of meat – into which I dunk pieces of Arabic bread. For the next course I eat it as a sauce poured over rice, with Egyptian Salad (see page 25). Others like to have it as a soup, with the meat that was cooked in it and some rice added to it, all seasoned with a dash of lemon juice. Still others cut up pieces of bread, moisten them with Melokheya, add rice and pour more on top. If the stock is made with a whole goose or chicken, these are removed, browned in the oven and served separately.

If you are using fresh 'melokheya', the preparation is slightly different. For the quantities here you would need about 750 g [$1\frac{1}{2}$ lb] of fresh leaves. You can also use half fresh and half dried, which saves expense and some of the labour of preparation, and still gives a superior flavour. Wash the 'melokheya', shake off excess water, strip the leaves from the stems (which should be discarded) and spread the leaves out on a cloth to dry thoroughly, which takes several hours. Then chop them finely: the traditional tool is a half-moon cutter, but a food processor does it much more easily.

1 Make the broth with the ingredients on the left, following the method on page 38. Simmer for about 2 hours or until the meat is very tender. (In a pressure cooker it takes 25 to 30 minutes.) Leave to cool, then remove all the fat.
2 Crush the dried *melokheya* leaves to a powder, preferably in a blender or food processor. There should be enough powder to completely fill a large teacup or mug. Put in a large bowl, take a ladleful or two of the cold stock and pour it on to the powdered *melokheya*. This restores its fresh flavour.
3 Bring the stock to the boil in a very large saucepan. (The *melokheya* swells when cooked.) Add the soaked *melokheya* mixture to the stock and stir thoroughly to mix it in. Bring to a slow boil and cook, half covered, for about 45 minutes. Stir from time to time and check that nothing is sticking to the bottom of the pan. A good beating is also necessary, particularly when using dried *melokheya*, as the soup tends to separate. The ideal final result is a well-blended green soup.
4 Prepare the Ta'leya. Crush the garlic and fry quite briskly with the crushed coriander seed in clarified butter until you can smell the fragrance of the coriander. Add to the soup, with a squeeze of lemon juice if you like, just before serving.

The amount of Ta'leya varies according to individual preference, and some people also add ground cumin seed and cayenne pepper.

CROUTONS

I find that the traditional method of making *croûtons*, by frying cubes of stale bread in butter, makes them too rich, for they absorb an enormous amount of butter. I have devised a quick way of making lighter *croûtons* with a flavour of butter but using a fraction of the amount. Cut thick slices of bread and spread both sides with butter. Cut these into cubes and bake in a moderate oven, about 180°C [350°F, gas 4], until crisp.

FREEZING STOCK AND SAUCE

Homemade stock and tomato sauce can be frozen in an ice-cube tray, and the frozen cubes transferred to a plastic bag and kept in the freezer. These basic ingredients are then always available and ready for immediate use, no matter how little you need.

HARICOT BEAN SOUP

PREPARATION TIME
8 hours soaking
2¼ hours, including 2 hours
cooking

500 g [1 lb] **haricot beans**
15 ml [1 tbsp] **clarified butter**
1 large **onion**
salt and pepper to taste

TA'LEYA
3 cloves **garlic**
5 ml [1 tsp] **clarified butter**
5 ml [1 tsp] **crushed coriander
seed**
15 ml [1 tbsp] **paprika**
2.5 ml [½ tsp] **chilli powder**

TO SERVE
croûtons
lemon wedges
butter
**a few sprigs fresh parsley or
coriander, chopped**

(picture on page 41)

1 Rinse the beans in two or three changes of water, cover with water and leave to soak for at least 8 hours.
2 Melt the clarified butter in a saucepan. Chop the onion finely, add to the pan and soften over medium heat. When the onion is transparent, raise the heat and fry until golden, stirring continually. Add the beans with their soaking water. Bring to the boil, then lower the heat, half cover the pan and simmer for about 1½ hours. In a pressure cooker this will take only about 25 minutes.
3 When the beans are soft enough to be squashed with a fork, liquidize them with enough of the cooking liquid to give the consistency of a cream soup. Return to the pan and set over a low heat. You may need to add a little more liquid to thin the soup down to your liking. Bring to the boil, then reduce the heat to simmer and cook for about 30 minutes.
4 Prepare the Ta'leya. Chop the garlic very finely. Melt a teaspoonful of clarified butter in a small pan. When it is sizzling, add the garlic and coriander, paprika and chilli powder, stir and fry quickly for about half a minute, then tip into the soup. Ladle a little soup into the pan and stir to mix in the last fragments, then pour back into the saucepan. Add salt and pepper, taste and adjust the seasoning.
5 Serve with *croûtons*, and wedges of lemon and some butter on the side, since some people may like to add a little lemon juice, or a dab of butter in the French manner. Sprinkle the soup with a little chopped fresh parsley or coriander if you like.

Black-eyed beans can be used instead of haricot beans to make an equally fine soup.

TRAHANAS SOUP

The recipe for this splendid soup was taught me by a London Cypriot friend, Sylva Kofu. She insisted that it should be made with a plain broth of beef and marrow bones only, without any additions at all. Other people will swear that you need a good chicken broth with all the usual additions. I've tried both and like them equally; see what you think.

Trahanas comes in pieces or crushed. If halumi cheese is not available, mozzarella is an adequate substitute.

PREPARATION TIME
2 hours soaking
45 minutes, including 30
minutes cooking

½ teacupful **trahanas**
1.2 litres [2 pints] **broth (see
right)**
salt and pepper to taste
3–4 **tomatoes**
120 g [4 oz] **halumi cheese**

TO SERVE
lemon wedges

(picture on page 41)

1 If the trahanas is in pieces, crush it. Cover in water and soak for a couple of hours.
2 Bring the broth to the boil and add the soaked trahanas, stirring constantly until completely blended. The purpose is to thicken as well as flavour the soup. Add salt and pepper to taste. Skin and chop the tomatoes, add them and cook for about 30 minutes on a low heat (using a heat diffuser if possible), stirring occasionally.
3 Cut the halumi cheese into small cubes, add it to the soup, and cook for 5 minutes. The cheese should be melting but still holding its shape. Serve with wedges of lemon, as some people like to give the flavour an extra tang.

An Egyptian soup or stew would never be served without the soft, round, flat bread found throughout the Arab world. Traditionally the bread is never cut; pieces are torn off by hand and used to scoop up food from the plate. RIGHT Two Egyptian women making bread at home. The dough is shaped into large circles, then baked in a brick and clay oven.

FISH

No one, I think, will ever forget, even if they have enjoyed it only once, the aroma and flavour of a freshly caught Mediterranean fish grilled over charcoal. You may eat it in any of countless harbourside restaurants in Alexandria or Athens, Algiers or Istanbul. The succulent fish, redolent of the sea, needs only a hint of flavouring from a little garlic, lemon juice and olive oil to be perfect.

In the Middle East fish is also baked, with or without vegetables, and fried, either whole if small or medium-sized, or cut into slices or fillets if larger. There is a variety of sauces to accompany grilled, baked or fried fish (see pages 136–138). Fish make delicious stews and soups, and can also be braised in the style known as *sofrito*. They can be minced and made into loaves and rissoles cooked in tasty sauces. All these recipes can be applied to most locally available fish.

For a while it looked as if fresh fish was going to disappear completely from British shops. Very few fishmongers were left; but now fresh fish seems to be coming back. In the thirty-odd years I have lived in this country I have seen much change. When we first arrived, we could buy superb sea bass and sea bream as well as halibut and turbot, and the more common cod, hake, whiting, whitebait and so on. These first two were surprisingly cheap in comparison with other countries where they were high-priced delicacies. Oddly, that was the reason for their disappearance from the British market. Since then Britain has become increasingly cosmopolitan, and we are beginning to see the return of the fishmonger offering a wide variety of fish.

Grilled Freshwater Trout (*top*) and Baked Grey Mullet, served with Tahina Dip. Other classic sauces (pages 136–8) are also good with fish

45

The design of Turkish caïques, traditional Mediterranean fishing boats, has not changed since ancient times. ABOVE Dikili, a small fishing village on the Aegean coast. Turkish fish dishes rely on the superb quality of the fish, which is very often simply grilled over charcoal.

GRILLED AND BAKED FISH

There are a few very simple guiding principles for grilled and baked fish. First, while most types of fish can be grilled, they should be cooked in this way only if they are really fresh, with bright eyes and glistening skin. Small and medium-sized fish, such as sprats, fresh sardines, red and grey mullet, mackerel, snapper, small sea bass and sea bream, should be grilled whole. Larger fish, such as cod, halibut and hake, can be sliced into steaks, then marinated and grilled, as can fresh or frozen fillets.

Second, any fish that can be grilled can equally well be baked – and vice versa, always assuming absolute freshness. In the recipes that follow, any named fish can be changed for another whole fish, slice or fillet of the same size or type. I have given a few hints on the slight differences in procedure necessary when using steaks or fillets of larger fish instead of whole smaller fish. The various fish do differ in oiliness, and where this matters I have also mentioned it in the recipe. The important point is that all the recipes are for firm-fleshed fish.

To flavour fish in a Middle Eastern way, marinate it in lime or lemon juice and olive oil, with some garlic, maybe a piece of fresh ginger, fresh herbs such as parsley or fennel leaves, and salt or pepper. There is a simple guiding principle: the more delicate the fish, the more delicate the marinade should be.

Of course, a marinade is ideal for giving a Middle Eastern flavour to fish cooked on a barbecue. Fish can also be grilled on a lightly oiled cast-iron grill pan over a high heat – it works equally well on electric and gas cookers.

GRILLED FRESHWATER TROUT

PREPARATION TIME
45 minutes, including 15 minutes marinating and 15 minutes cooking

**4 river trout, each about 450 g [1 lb] before preparation
2 cloves garlic
60 ml [4 tbsp] chopped parsley
salt and pepper to taste
juice of 1 or 2 limes or lemons
15 ml [1 tbsp] olive oil
a few sprigs parsley, chopped**

TO GARNISH
lemon slices

(picture on page 44)

This is a perfect example of a local fish cooked in a Middle Eastern way.

1 Prepare the fish, or have it prepared, as described on page 48.
2 Cut a piece of foil for each fish to rest on. This will be a great help in turning them over during grilling. Make a couple of small cuts on each side of the fish and insert thin slivers of garlic. Chop the rest of the garlic, mix with the parsley and stuff the fish with it. Sprinkle the fish with salt, pepper and lime or lemon juice and rub this all over the fish with your hands. Leave to marinate for at least 15 minutes. Trout, being oily, do not require any oil at this stage.
3 Turn the grill up high. When it is very hot put each fish, on its foil, on the grill rack and cook on each side until the skin starts cracking, about 6 or 7 minutes a side in the case of fair-sized trout. If the fish seems to be drying up, squeeze on a little lemon juice, or any leftover marinade.
4 Pour the olive oil into a cup, add the chopped parsley and beat to combine. Spread half the mixture on the serving dish. Tip the cooked fish on to the dish, top with the rest of the mixture and garnish with lemon slices.

If you cook white fish in this way, add 15 ml [1 tbsp] oil to the marinade.

Fresh coriander or fennel leaves can be used instead of parsley. Also, if you have some Preserved Lemons (see page 139), you can cut them into small pieces and add them to the stuffing, and use the liquid from the preserve instead of lemon juice – but remember that it is rather salty, so omit salt from the marinade.

BAKED GREY MULLET

PREPARATION TIME
1 hour 10 minutes, including 30 minutes marinating and 30 minutes cooking

**1 grey mullet, about 1.5 kg [or 3 lb] before preparation
1 medium onion
3–4 cloves garlic
1 large green pepper
45–60 ml [3–4 tbsp] chopped parsley
juice of 1 lemon
salt and pepper to taste
30–45 ml [2–3 tbsp] olive oil**

TO GARNISH
lemon wedges

(picture on page 46)

When baking fish, the larger the fish, the better value it is. Ask your fishmonger not to cut off the head and tail and to gut it through the smallest possible incision.

1 Wash the fish and remove any remaining scales.
2 Choose a baking dish that will take the fish whole. Slice the onion very thinly and spread it over the dish.
3 Chop most of the garlic very finely and cut the pepper into the thinnest possible strips. Mix well in a bowl with the parsley, lemon juice, salt and pepper. Stir in the oil. Pour most of this mixture over the onions, but reserve just enough to put inside the fish – to flavour it, it isn't meant to be a full-scale stuffing.
4 Cut one or two slits on each side of the fish and insert slivers of garlic. Spoon the reserved mixture inside the fish. Put it on the dish and turn it over and over so that it gets coated with the marinade. Leave in a cool place for at least 30 minutes.
* The dish may be prepared in advance to this point, covered with cling film or foil and stored in the refrigerator.
5 Preheat the oven fairly hot, 190°C [375°F, gas 5]. Bake the fish, basting it a couple of times and turning it once after 20 minutes. It should be done in about 30 minutes, but check a little earlier.
6 Serve garnished with lemon wedges with the cooked marinade as a sauce.

Whole fish are very good marinated in a simple mixture of olive oil, lemon juice, salt and pepper, served with Egg and Lemon Sauce (page 136), Tahina Dip (page 16) or mayonnaise. It can be covered with the sauce and garnished with parsley, pine nuts, paprika, olives or anything that you feel is suitable.

FISH BAKED WITH VEGETABLES A whole fish can be marinated as described above, and baked on a bed of sliced potatoes, onions, tomatoes and peppers. The marinade can be flavoured with thyme, oregano, bay or fennel leaves. But don't overdo the mixture of herbs: it is better to have two or three in harmony than a cacophony.

BAKED FISH FILLETS OR STEAKS Fish fillets can also be baked in any of the above ways. They are also good baked in a cooked sauce, such as the basic Tomato Sauce on page 137. Reduce the sauce until quite thick, cover the fillets with the sauce, wrap in foil and bake as above.

STUFFED SEA BASS

PREPARATION TIME

1½ hours, including 1 hour
  cooking

1 sea bass, at least 1 kg [or 2¼
  lb] before preparation
80 g [3 oz] fine soft
  breadcrumbs
6–10 olives, depending on size
60 g [2 oz] coarsely ground
  walnuts
60 ml [4 tbsp] chopped parsley
15 ml [1 tbsp] tomato purée
salt and pepper to taste
5 ml [1 tsp] paprika
5 ml [1 tsp] turmeric
5 ml [1 tsp] ground allspice
1 large onion
juice of 2 lemons
6 tomatoes, or a 400 g [14 oz]
  can
30–45 ml [2–3 tbsp] olive oil
30–45 ml [2–3 tbsp] fish stock
  (optional)
a dot chilli powder

TO GARNISH (optional)
small sprigs parsley
lemon slices
olives

I first saw a fish boned through the back, with superb skill, at a demonstration of West Indian food by the professional cook Rosamond Grant. Your fishmonger may be able to bone a fish in this way; but if not, with a little practice and following the step-by-step instructions below, you should be able to do it yourself.

1 Wash and descale the fish thoroughly.

2 Prepare the stuffing. Quickly crisp the breadcrumbs in a dry frying pan. Put them in a bowl. Stone the olives, cut into small pieces and add to the bowl with the walnuts and some of the parsley. Add tomato purée, salt, pepper, paprika, turmeric and allspice. Grate about 2 tablespoonfuls off the onion into the bowl. Add the juice of one lemon, mix throughly and adjust the seasoning to your taste.

3 Bone and gut the fish, rinse and dry it, put in as much stuffing as it will comfortably hold and sew it up. (See the diagrams for guidance.) Reserve any spare stuffing.

4 Preheat the oven to moderate, 180°C [350°F, gas 4]. Choose an ovenproof dish that will take the fish whole. Slice the rest of the onions and spread out in the dish. Chop the tomatoes if fresh, or drain and crush if canned. Reserve the liquid from the can. Add the tomatoes to the dish and sprinkle with the rest of the chopped parsley and any remaining stuffing.

5 Mix the olive oil in a jug with the fish stock if you have any, or some of the liquid from the canned tomatoes, or water. Add the juice of the other lemon: there should be a generous half teacupful of liquid in all. Also add salt, pepper, and a small pinch of chilli powder. Beat well and pour half of it on to the dish. Lay the fish on the bed of vegetables and pour the rest of the liquid over it.

6 Bake the fish for about 1 hour in all, basting after 30 minutes. When it is cooked, taste the sauce and adjust the seasoning if necessary. Serve with the sauce spooned over. If you like, garnish it with sprigs of parsley along the spine of the fish, thin slices of lemon and whole olives. It will look superb and taste even better.

You can vary the herb and spice combination in the stuffing by adding to or replacing those listed with, for example, a little ground cumin seed and a dot of harissa or chilli sauce or powder, and adding small pieces of Perserved Lemon (see page 139).

BONING A FISH THROUGH THE BACK

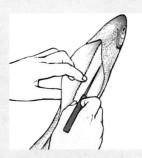   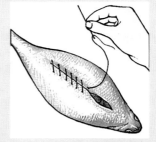

1 Using a sharp knife, cut along each side of the backbone.

2 Ease out the backbone, snip it with scissors at the tail and head ends, and remove it completely. Remove the guts.

3 Remove the gills and wash the fish in cold running water.

4 After stuffing, sew up the slit with a needle and thread.

BUYING AND SCALING FISH

If you are going to cook your fish whole or stuffed, make sure that the fishmonger leaves on the head, and if he is gutting it for you try to make him do this through the smallest possible incision so that the fish retain its shape.

    Always make sure that there are no scales left on a fish (there often are). Using the blunt back of a knife, scrape off the scales, working towards the head.

Small Fried Fish and Stuffed Sea Bass with a spicy tomato and herb stuffing

SMALL FRIED FISH

Fresh sardines (larger than the canned ones) or small red mullet are ideal for this dish. Allow two sardines or one mullet per person.

1 Wash, descale and gut the fish if necessary.

2 Chop the garlic very finely and mix with the cumin seed and parsley, salt and pepper. Stuff the fish with about half the mixture. Rub the rest on the outside, and leave for at least 30 minutes in a cool place, or covered in the refrigerator, for the fish to take up the flavour.

3 Coat the fish with flour and shake off the excess. Heat enough oil for semi-deep frying in a heavy pan or wok. Test the oil by adding a pinch of breadcrumbs. As soon as they sizzle to the surface the oil is hot enough. Fry the fish for 5 to 10 minutes, or until cooked. Serve either hot or cold with wedges of lemon.

Slices or steaks of larger fish such as sea bream, grey mullet or sea bass can be cooked in the same way. Coat the slices with the mixture and leave to stand as above. Then moisten them with beaten egg, dip in flour and fry. They can be served with Egg and Lemon Sauce (see page 136), Tahina Dip (see page 16) or mayonnaise.

PREPARATION TIME
50–55 minutes, including 30
minutes marinating and
5–10 minutes cooking

4 fresh small red mullet, or 8
fresh sardines
2 cloves garlic
2 ml [scant ½ tsp] ground
cumin seed
45 ml [3 tbsp] finely chopped
parsley
salt and pepper to taste
flour for coating
oil for semi-deep frying

TO GARNISH
lemon wedges

SLICED FISH IN TOMATO SAUCE

PREPARATION TIME

1½ hours, including 50 minutes
  cooking

1.5 kg [or 3 lb] white fish, e.g.
  cod, hake or halibut (see
  right)
1 egg
about 60 ml [4 tbsp] dry
  breadcrumbs
1 large onion
oil for semi-deep frying
15 ml [1 tbsp] water
1 clove garlic
45 ml [3 tbsp] chopped parsley
1 400 g [14 oz] can tomatoes
salt and pepper to taste
15 ml [1 tbsp] tomato purée
15 ml [1 tbsp] vinegar
5 ml [1 tsp] sugar, or to taste
  (optional)

This is a delicious way of preparing large, firm fish. The piquant tomato sauce suits both a plain white fish such as cod or hake, or halibut, turbot, grey mullet or sea bass. Buy steaks, or cut the fish into slices about 2 cm [¾ in.] thick.

1 Slice the fish if necessary, dry it and dip in beaten egg and coat with breadcrumbs. Chop the onion very finely. Pour oil into a heavy sautéing pan, large enough to hold the fish in one layer, with fairly high sides and a lid, to a depth of about 3 cm [1 in.]. Heat it quite hot: test by dropping in a pinch of breadcrumbs, which should sizzle up to the surface. Fry the fish slices quickly until brown on both sides. Remove them and drain on kitchen paper.
2 Carefully pour away most of the oil, leaving just enough in the pan to coat it well. Reduce the heat to medium, add the onion and cook until transparent. If some of the breadcrumbs left in the pan stick, scrape them off with a spoon and mix with the onion. Add a tablespoon of water or juice from the can of tomatoes, bring to the boil, then reduce the heat to simmer. Meanwhile chop the garlic and add to the pan with the parsley.
3 Drain and add the tomatoes and mash them with a fork, then add salt, pepper, tomato purée and vinegar. Stir and taste: you may like to add a little sugar. Bring to the boil, then reduce the heat and simmer for 15 to 20 minutes.
4 Add the fish slices, turning them over to coat them with the sauce. If the sauce is too thick, dilute it with some water or juice from the can, or a little more vinegar if needed. Cover the pan and simmer for about 20 minutes. This dish is best served with rice.

You can also use the Tomato Sauce on page 137, if you have some already made. Warm it up and add fresh parsley and, if you like, some fresh coriander. You might also add small pieces of Preserved Lemon or a dot of chilli powder. Fry the fish in a separate pan, add it to the sauce and simmer for about 20 minutes.

ESCABECHE

PREPARATION TIME

30 minutes, including 25
  minutes cooking
2 days marinating

1.5–2 kg [3–4 lb] fish, e.g. 4
  mackerel (or see right)
flour for coating
15–30 ml [1–2 tbsp] oil, +
  more for semi-deep frying
2 medium onions
1 large green pepper
2–3 cloves garlic
a pinch cayenne pepper
20 ml [1 rounded tbsp] whole
  allspice
45 ml [3 tbsp] chopped parsley
a pinch dried thyme
2 bay leaves
salt and pepper to taste
1 teacupful vinegar

Various versions of this dish of marinated or quickly pickled fish are found all around the Mediterranean under various names; another one is 'scabetch'. It has even crossed the Atlantic to Jamaica, where it is called 'escovitch', and to South America, where a version made with completely raw fish (but 'cooked' by the acid marinade) is known as 'ceviche'. The recipe I have given here is for my favourite version, which is splendid made with mackerel; you can use almost any small or medium-sized, firm-textured whole fish, from large sardines to smallish sea bream or John Dory. Larger fish can be sliced and cooked in the same way, too. The dish improves with a little keeping in the refrigerator, and should be made at least two days in advance.

1 Wash, scale and gut the fish as necessary. Dry and roll in flour.
2 Put a little oil in a frying pan and set it over medium heat. Finely slice the onions, add them to the pan and let them cook gently while you cut the pepper into strips and chop the garlic. Add these with the cayenne pepper, whole allspice, parsley, a little dried thyme rubbed in your hands to release the flavour, bay leaves, salt and pepper and vinegar. Bring to simmering point and cook for 10 to 15 minutes.
3 Meanwhile fry the fish in about 3 cm [1 in.] depth of oil in a separate pan until golden brown, and put it on kitchen paper. Transfer it to a deepish dish. Pour the sauce over it and leave to cool. Cover and leave it in the refrigerator for at least 2 days. Serve cold.

You can also cook the dish in one pan, if you prefer. Fry the fish first, then remove it from the pan and pour most of the oil away. Add the onions to the pan and continue making the sauce as above.

Here are a few tips for recognizing a really fresh fish. Its eyes should be bright, the skin should be shiny and the area under the gills should be red. The fish should be firm to the touch and smell of the sea.

Left to right Sliced Fish in Tomato Sauce, Fish Sofrito, made here with monkfish, and Escabeche, served with a special Rice for Fish (*recipe on page 104*)

FISH SOFRITO

PREPARATION TIME
20–30 minutes, including 15
 minutes cooking

30 ml [2 tbsp] oil
1 clove garlic
juice of 1 lemon
2.5 ml [$\frac{1}{2}$ tsp] turmeric
75 ml [5 tbsp] fish stock or
 water
4 slices monkfish, each about
 200 g [7 oz]

TO GARNISH
a few sprigs parsley, chopped

This is a delicious and very quick way to cook fillets, slices or steaks of large fish. I like it best made with monkfish, but I've also cooked a much coarser fish, conger eel, in this way with good results. It may be eaten hot or cold. If you use good fish stock rather than water for the sauce, it will set to a delicious jelly when it cools.

1 Choose a frying pan which will take all the fish in one layer, and pour in just enough oil to coat the base. Slice the garlic very finely, add it to the pan with the lemon juice, turmeric and a little water, and bring very gently to the boil.
2 Meanwhile, wash and dry the fish. Raise the heat, and add the fish to the pan when the liquid is just beginning to tremble. Add the fish stock if you have some, or otherwise water, to just cover the fish. Bring it to simmering point and cook very gently until done, which will be no more than 10 minutes.
3 Transfer the fish to a deep dish. The sauce should be quite thick; if not, reduce it before pouring it over the fish. Sprinkle with chopped parsley.

51

FISH LOAF SOFRITO

PREPARATION TIME
1 hour, including 40 minutes
   cooking

450 g [1 lb] **fish fillets**
   (haddock, hake or cod)
1 **large onion**
1 **clove garlic**
about 120 g [4 oz] **soft**
   breadcrumbs
salt and pepper to taste
5 ml [1 tsp] **ground cumin**
2.5 ml [½ tsp] **turmeric**
oil for generous shallow frying

SOFRITO SAUCE
about 30 ml [2 tbsp] **oil, if not**
   using oil from frying loaves
1 **clove garlic**
juice of 1 lemon
2.5 ml [½ tsp] **turmeric**
1 **teacupful fish stock or water**

This delicious fish loaf is an example of a traditional dish which used to be time-consuming and messy to prepare but, when made with a modern gadget such as a food processor, presents no such problems. The 'sofrito' sauce, made as in the previous recipe, is used to cook the fish loaf in. The dish is excellent as part of a buffet spread.

1 Mince the fish finely: it will be easier if you poach it a little first. Finely chop or grate the onion and garlic. Mix most of the breadcrumbs well with the fish. (If you are using a food processor, first chop the onion and garlic, then add the breadcrumbs and the fish and process until all is well mixed.) Add salt, pepper, cumin and turmeric, mix again and check the consistency is just firm enough to handle.

2 Transfer the mixture to a mixing bowl. Taste and adjust the seasoning if necessary. Knead it with your hands (see page 77). If it is too soft to be formed into a roll, stiffen it with more breadcrumbs. Damp your hands slightly, take half the mixture and form it into a roll about 5 cm [2 in.] thick and as evenly cylindrical as possible – but don't worry if it is a bit thicker in the middle. Make a second roll with the rest of the mixture.

3 Fry the two loaves in fairly hot oil, turning them, for a few minutes or until lightly browned all over. Remove from the pan and drain on kitchen paper.

4 Use a frying pan (or a saucepan in which both loaves will fit comfortably) to prepare the *sofrito* sauce in the same way as in the previous recipe. (You can use the pan and oil from frying the loaves if you like, but remember to pour away most of the oil.) Adjust the sauce to a fairly thin liquid with fish stock if available, or water if not. There should be about a teacupful of sauce. Put in the two loaves and poach gently. Shake and tilt the pan from time to time to spread the liquid around, and turn the loaves over. Cook them for about 30 minutes.

5 Remove the loaves from the pan and leave to cool. Cut them into slices about 2 cm [¾ in.] thick and arrange them on a dish. Reheat the sauce, reduce it until thick and pour it over the slices.

* The dish may be prepared in advance to this stage. Store in the refrigerator until shortly before serving.

FISH BALLS IN TOMATO SAUCE

PREPARATION TIME
45 minutes, including 20
   minutes cooking

450 g [1 lb] **fish fillets**
   (haddock, hake or cod)
120 g [4 oz] **soft breadcrumbs,**
   or more if needed
a few sprigs fresh coriander,
   chopped
5 ml [1 tsp] **ground cinnamon**
salt and pepper to taste

SAUCE
about 30 ml [2 tbsp] **oil**
1 **medium onion**
6 **tomatoes, or a 400 g [14 oz]**
   can
1 **fresh chilli**
1 **clove garlic**
salt and pepper to taste
5 ml [1 tsp] **ground cumin seed**
1 **teacupful water**
15 ml [1 tbsp] **paprika**
2.5 ml [½ tsp] **turmeric**

These fish balls are made from a very similar mixture to that used for the fish loaf in the previous recipe.

1 Mince the fish finely, and add the breadcrumbs, fresh coriander, cinnamon, salt and pepper. Mix well. Add extra breadcrumbs if the mixture is too soft, and form it into round rissoles the size of a marble, or little finger shapes if you prefer (see page 77).

2 Choose a frying pan that will take all the fish balls in one layer, and pour in just enough oil to coat the base of the pan. Grate in the onion. Finely chop the tomatoes, reserving the liquid if using canned tomatoes, and add to the heated pan. Bring the liquid to the boil, then lower the heat to medium and leave to cook for a while.

3 Meanwhile, deseed the chilli and chop it very finely. Chop the garlic finely. Add these, with salt, pepper and cumin, to a teacupful of water or tomato liquid, and pour into the pan. Add the paprika and turmeric. Bring back to the boil, then lower the heat to simmer.

4 Gently roll the fish balls into the sauce and poach gently for about 15 minutes. Serve on a bed of rice.

The fish balls can also be coated in dried breadcrumbs and fried separately until golden, before adding them to the sauce.

The sauce in this recipe goes equally well with the Fish Loaf above, while the *sofrito* sauce in that recipe can replace the tomato sauce for the fish balls.

Fish Stew piled over a mound of couscous, with the rest in a separate bowl (*back left*), Fish Loaf Sofrito (*front*) and Fish Balls in Tomato Sauce (*right*)

FISH STEW FOR COUSCOUS

PREPARATION TIME
1 hour, including cooking

30 ml [2 tbsp] oil
1 large onion
2 cloves garlic
1 400 g [14 oz] can tomatoes
salt to taste
5 ml [1 tsp] ground cumin seed
5 ml [1 tsp] cayenne pepper
5 ml [1 tsp] turmeric
15 ml [1 tbsp] tomato purée
1 large green pepper
4 small potatoes
2 teacupfuls water
2 fresh sardines (or sprats)
2 small mackerel
250 g [½ lb] monkfish
450 g [1 lb] couscous

I have eaten this stew as part of a whole fish meal – brik, fish soup and couscous – cooked by a young Tunisian friend in London. She chose the fish from a selection at the local fishmonger. Although couscous, the national dish of the North African countries, is usually associated with meat stews, the Tunisians also cook it with fish. The other North Africans tease them by calling them the 'fish couscous eaters'. In fact, in some regions of Algeria bordering on Tunisia you can also find fish couscous.

1 Put the oil in the bottom part of a couscous steamer or in a large, heavy-based pan and set over medium heat. Finely chop the onion and garlic and add. Drain the canned tomatoes, chop them and add to the pan when the onion begins to brown. Add salt, all the spices and the tomato purée to the mixture. Bring to simmering point and leave to cook with the pan half covered.

2 Cut the green pepper into large pieces, discarding the seeds. Leave the potatoes whole, peeled or with their skins on, as you prefer. Add both to the mixture with a couple of teacupfuls of water, bring to the boil then simmer for about 15 minutes. Meanwhile, prepare the fish. Gut the sardines but leave them whole. Cut the mackerel into halves, discarding the heads, and cut the monkfish into large chunks.

3 When the vegetables are cooked, remove them and keep warm. Add enough water to the pan to cover the fish. Bring to the boil, put in the fish, cover and simmer till the fish is done, about 30 minutes. Return the vegetables. Following the instructions for couscous on page 108, give it the second steaming over the fish stew.

4 Taste and adjust the seasoning if necessary. Serve the fish and vegetables on a mound of couscous with the rest of the stew in a separate bowl.

This fish stew goes equally well with rice. You can vary it by adding other vegetables at the appropriate time so that they are all ready together: carrots near the start of cooking, courgettes near the end, and so on.

POULTRY

Chicken, poussin, duck, goose, turkey, pigeon and quail, cooked in a thousand and one different ways, are popular throughout the Middle East. Young, tender birds are simply grilled. Larger fowl are made into stews with vegetables, fragrant with herbs and spices and often enriched with dried fruits. They are stuffed before being casseroled, roasted or steamed, and are also made into spectacular festive dishes.

Apart from quickly grilled dishes, most of the traditional recipes call for long, slow cooking so that by the time the fowl is tender, the liquid and accompanying ingredients will have developed their full flavour. However, modern battery chickens tend to cook in a fraction of this time. Unless otherwise stated, the cooking times given apply to these birds. For this reason I often stipulate that if the chicken is done before the sauce has attained its full richness, you should take out the bird while you cook and reduce the sauce until it no longer 'tastes of water'. It is also often advisable, for instance when using chicken pieces rather than a whole bird, to make the sauce to a midway stage, and then add the chicken, having first fried it if appropriate.

If you can, buy free-range corn or grain-fed chickens. Fortunately, we are beginning to see the return of these 'real' birds. They take longer to cook than factory-farmed birds; if you do use one, increase the cooking times given in the following recipes accordingly. When you are cooking a chicken whole and you want to know if it is cooked through, stick a sharp knife into the centre of the thigh: there should be no trace of pinkness.

Chicken Sofrito (*top left*), Chicken Tajine with Olives and Lemon (*bottom left*) and Grilled Poussins, with a chopped mixed Pepper Salad (*recipe on page 20*)

55

Raisins are used in savoury dishes – pilafs, stuffed vegetables, chilled soups or cooked with meat or poultry – throughout the Middle East. ABOVE The vineyards and distinctive cone dwellings of Cappadocia, centuries ago a volcanic region and now one of the three main wine-producing areas of Turkey.

CHICKEN TAJINE WITH RAISINS AND ALMONDS

PREPARATION TIME
2 hours, including 1½ hours cooking

1 medium chicken, about
 1.5 kg [3 lb]
30 ml [2 tbsp] oil
salt and pepper to taste
a few strands saffron (or a pinch turmeric)
10 ml [2 tsp] ground ginger
5 ml [1 tsp] ground cinnamon
2 medium onions
200 ml [7 fl oz] water
60 g [2 oz] peeled almonds

RAISIN SAUCE
3–4 medium onions
30–60 g [1–2 oz] raisins
60 g [2 oz] butter
5 ml [1 tsp] ground cinnamon
10 ml [2 tsp] sugar
15 ml [1 tbsp] water

1 Joint the chicken and put the pieces in a large, heavy-based saucepan with a couple of tablespoons of oil, salt, pepper, saffron, ginger and cinnamon. Finely chop the onions and add to the pan. Set it over a medium heat, half cover it and cook for about 30 minutes, turning the chicken from time to time.

2 Add a teacupful of water, bring to the boil, and lower the heat to simmer half covered for a further 30 minutes until just cooked.

3 Make the raisin sauce. Chop the onions very finely and put in a smaller saucepan with the raisins, butter, cinnamon, sugar and a little water. Cook uncovered on a medium heat, stirring from time to time, for about 45 minutes or until the onions have melted away and the whole mixture becomes thick, glossy and golden brown. If the sauce is thick enough but the onions are still visible, add a little more water and continue cooking until they disappear.

4 Add the almonds to the chicken and carry on simmering until it is tender. Arrange the pieces on a dish (or in a *tajine* pot if you have one) and pour the sauce over them, arranging the almonds on top. Serve the raisin sauce in a separate bowl.

CHICKEN TAJINE WITH PRUNES AND SESAME SEEDS Cook the chicken as above, but use prunes instead of raisins for the sauce, and roasted sesame seeds instead of almonds. Cook the prunes with a little liquid from the chicken and the other ingredients for the sauce. Gently dry roast a handful of sesame seeds. To serve, pour the sauce over the chicken, arrange any whole prunes on the top and sprinkle with sesame seeds.

CHICKEN SOFRITO WITH POTATOES

PREPARATION TIME
2 hours, including 1½ hours
  cooking

30 ml [2 tbsp] oil
5 ml [1 tsp] turmeric
3–4 cloves garlic
juice of 2–3 lemons
300 ml [10 fl oz] good stock, or
  more as required
1 medium chicken, about
  1.5 kg [3 lb]
salt and pepper to taste
700 g [1½ lb] potatoes
oil for deep frying

TO GARNISH
a few sprigs parsley, chopped

(picture on page 54)

This very simple way of cooking chicken is a great favourite of mine. Both this recipe and the one below can easily be adapted for veal. The best cut to use is the knuckle, but instead of having it cut into slices, osso buco style, it is better to bone it and cut it into chunks with the marrow bone added separately for extra flavour. It should be tender enough to cut with a fork and will take a good 2 hours to cook.

1 Choose a heavy-based saucepan or flameproof casserole into which the whole chicken will fit comfortably. Pour in a thin layer of oil, add the turmeric, whole cloves of garlic, lemon juice and a large cupful of stock, and set over medium heat. Put in the chicken, sprinkle it with salt and pepper, and turn it over to coat it with the contents of the pan. Leave it breast down and cook, half covered, on medium heat, for about 1 hour. Turn from time to time, and add more stock if necessary to keep at least 3 cm [1 in.] of liquid in the casserole.
2 Preheat the oven to 200°C [400°F, gas 6]. Transfer the chicken to a roasting pan and put it in the oven to brown, about 30 minutes.
3 Cook the potatoes. Peel them and leave them whole if small; if large, cut into chunks or chips. Deep fry them until golden but not cooked through. Drain on kitchen paper, put them in the casserole and shake well to coat with liquid. Continue cooking until the potatoes are done. This should not take very long: check after about 5 minutes.
4 When the chicken is nicely browned, serve it with the potatoes in the sauce around it. A sprinkling of chopped parsley brings out the colour.

Although it gives an attractive finish, it is not necessary to brown the chicken in the oven. Instead, the whole dish can be cooked on top of the stove: add the fried potatoes to the cooked chicken, shake the casserole and simmer briefly until the potatoes are cooked.

Chicken pieces can also be cooked in this way, without the potatoes. Serve with rice instead.

COLD CHICKEN SOFRITO A chicken, cooked in a casserole as above, but without the potatoes, can be jointed when done, and the pieces skinned and arranged in a shallow bowl. Reduce the liquid in the casserole to a thick consistency and pour it over the chicken. When it cools it will form a delicious jelly.

CHICKEN TAJINE WITH OLIVES AND LEMON

PREPARATION TIME
1 hour 50 minutes, including
  1¾ hours cooking

1 medium chicken, about
  1.5 kg [3 lb], with giblets
  (optional)
30 ml [2 tbsp] oil
2 medium onions
1 clove garlic
1 lemon
a few strands saffron (or a
  pinch turmeric)
10 ml [2 tsp] ground ginger
salt and pepper to taste
45 ml [3 tbsp] chopped parsley
50–250 g [2–10 oz] green
  olives (according to taste)

(picture on page 54)

This and the 'tajine' recipe opposite were given to me by Fatima Ma'toughi. However, I have adapted them both by drastically reducing the amount of oil.

1 Pour enough oil into a heavy-based saucepan or flameproof casserole to coat the bottom. Put in the whole chicken. Grate the onions, crush the garlic and slice the lemon. Add with the saffron, ginger, salt and pepper. Turn the chicken over to coat it with the mixture and set over a medium heat, then cover the pan and cook for about 30 minutes, turning several times. If the mixture becomes dry, add a little water.
2 Add the chopped parsley and the olives (the number of olives depends on your taste). If you have the giblets, chop them into small pieces and add. Cook for another 45 minutes or so, turning from time to time, until the chicken is cooked through.
3 Preheat the oven to medium, 190°C [375°F, gas 5]. Transfer the chicken to a roasting pan or ovenproof serving dish and put it in the oven to brown, about another 30 minutes.
4 Reduce the mixture remaining in the pan to a thick sauce. To serve, pour the sauce over and around the chicken and arrange the lemon slices on top.
* The chicken can be cooked in advance and reheated and browned in the oven. Reheat the sauce separately and serve as above.

If you have a Preserved Lemon (see page 139) use half of it, chopped, instead of the sliced lemon, but add to the chicken with the parsley (step 2).

Chicken Tajine with Raisins and Almonds and Chicken with a Rich Burghul Stuffing

GRILLED POUSSINS

PREPARATION TIME
1 hour 5 minutes, including 30
  minutes marinating and 30
  minutes cooking

2 poussins
1–2 cloves garlic
salt and pepper to taste
juice of 1 lemon
30 ml [2 tbsp] olive oil

(picture on page 54)

Like fish, tender, delicate-flavoured poussins are eminently suited to grilling, either in the open on charcoal (see pages 78–79) or by more prosaic indoor methods.

1   Split the poussins open down the back and flatten them by beating with the flat side of a cleaver or a rolling pin. If they are large, remove the legs. Slice the garlic thinly. Put the poussins (including the legs, if you have removed them) in a shallow bowl, sprinkle with salt and pepper, add the garlic, pour over most of the lemon juice and turn them to make sure they are evenly coated. Pour on a couple of tablespoonfuls of oil and leave to marinate in the refrigerator for at least 30 minutes, or several hours if more convenient.
2   Heat a cast-iron grill pan until it is really hot. Put the poussins on it and press them down well so that they make good contact with it. After about 5 minutes turn them over, press down again and grill for a few more minutes on a high heat. Reduce the heat to medium and cook for about another 10 minutes; turn and give the other side 10 minutes or until the inside of the leg is done. Transfer the poussins to a serving dish. Deglaze the grill pan with a little water and a squeeze of lemon juice. Pour the liquid over the poussins and sprinkle with a little more salt. Serve with rice or chipped potatoes, and a green salad.

Farm pigeons and quails are also delicious split, marinated and grilled in this way. Naturally you will need more of the smaller birds. Breast of chicken or turkey can also be marinated and grilled for a couple of minutes on each side; served with a generous green salad, this makes an interesting, quickly prepared lunch – and a low-calorie one for slimmers.

STUFFED POULTRY

Stuffed poultry is a great favourite in the Middle East. The main ingredients are usually rice, burghul or couscous with a great variety of additions: nuts and dried fruits, herbs, spices and sautéed liver and hearts, subtly flavoured or spicy to complement the bird.

CHICKEN WITH A RICH BURGHUL STUFFING

PREPARATION TIME
1 hour soaking
2½ hours, including 1½ hours
 cooking

1 medium roasting chicken,
 about 1.5 kg [3 lb]
250 g [½ lb] burghul
100 g [3½ oz] pine nuts
3 medium onions
5 ml [1 tsp] ground cinnamon
90 ml [6 tbsp] finely chopped
 parsley
80 g [3 oz] raisins
salt and pepper to taste
15–30 ml [1–2 tbsp] oil
1–2 oranges
30 g [1 oz] butter
15–30 ml [1–2 tbsp] clarified
 butter

TO GARNISH
orange slices (optional)

1 Soak the burghul in plenty of cold water for at least 1 hour.
2 Squeeze the burghul dry in a cloth and put it in a mixing bowl. Dry fry the pine nuts gently till lightly coloured and add. Chop one of the onions very finely. Add to the burghul with the cinnamon, parsley, raisins, salt and pepper. Mix well and check the seasoning. If the additions look sparse, add more: you can make the stuffing as rich as you like.
3 Chop the remaining onions very finely. Choose a saucepan or flameproof casserole into which the chicken will fit comfortably and pour in just enough oil to coat the base of the pan. Cook the onion gently until transparent. Squeeze one of the oranges, add the juice and simmer gently.
4 Stuff the chicken with as much of the burghul mixture as it will hold, adding small pieces of the butter. Put some stuffing under the breast skin. Reserve the remaining mixture. Sew up the bird if necessary.
5 Put the chicken in the pan and add enough water to come about halfway up the bird. Bring to the boil, lower the heat to simmer and cover the pan. Cook for about 1½ hours, or until the chicken is brown and the sauce thick and golden brown. Turn it over carefully from time to time and add a little more water if it is drying up.
6 Fry the remaining burghul mixture in very hot clarified butter, tossing it, for less than a minute. (A small wok is ideal for this, as you need less butter.)
7 Remove the chicken, carve it and keep warm. Tip the fried burghul into the pan, mix well with the liquid and set over a low heat. Taste the sauce in the pan, correct the seasoning and add more orange juice if you like. If the orange juice is sour, add a little sugar to the sauce.
8 To serve, pile all the burghul mixture in the serving dish and arrange the pieces of chicken on it. Garnish with orange slices if you like.

STEAMED STUFFED CHICKEN

PREPARATION TIME
3 hours 20 minutes, including
 2½ hours cooking

1.6 kg [3½ lb] chicken
2 sticks celery
3 spring onions
½ Preserved Lemon, or 5 ml [1
 tsp] dried lime, or juice of 1
 lemon
3–4 small tomatoes
15 ml [1 tbsp] tomato purée
a teacupful finely chopped
 parsley
salt and pepper to taste
5 ml [1 tsp] chilli powder
30 g [1 oz] butter
flour and water paste to seal
 steamer (see right)

TO SERVE
salt, pepper and ground cumin
 seed mixed to taste

(picture on page 61)

If you own a double steamer, you will be able to enjoy making this delicious Moroccan dish. Its subtlety of flavour calls for a good-quality chicken, such as one of the free-range, grain-fed birds which are now becoming more readily available.

1 Prepare the stuffing. Finely chop the celery, spring onions (including the green tops), lemon or lime (if used) and the tomatoes. Mix these together and add the tomato purée, parsley, salt, pepper, lemon juice (if used) and chilli powder, and the butter cut into small pieces. If you have the chicken liver and heart, chop into small pieces and add to the stuffing.
2 Fill the bottom of the steamer with plenty of water (but it must not touch the upper part when it boils). Bring to the boil while you stuff the chicken with the mixture and sew it up if necessary. Insert some stuffing under the breast skin. When the water boils put the top on the steamer, lower the heat and carefully seal the join between top and bottom with flour and water paste. Put the chicken, breast down, in the top of the steamer, cover with a clean damp cloth and put on the lid. Steam for 2 to 2½ hours, or until the chicken is cooked.
3 To serve, joint the chicken, arrange the pieces around the edge of a dish and spoon the stuffing into the centre. Sprinkle with the salt, pepper and cumin mixture.

If you are skilled at boning a whole chicken you can, of course, stuff and cook it in this way, reducing the cooking time accordingly.

GREEK CHICKEN PIE

PREPARATION TIME
3 hours, including 2 hours 20 minutes cooking
2 hours cooling and reheating

SERVES 8

500 g [1 lb] leeks
300 g [10 oz] butter
1 medium chicken, about 1.5 kg [3 lb], jointed
salt and pepper to taste
60 ml [4 tbsp] flour
450 ml [16 fl oz] milk
120 g [4 oz] grated Cheddar or other medium-strong cheese
4 eggs
a pinch ground nutmeg
250 g [½ lb] fila pastry

This is my friend Mireille Attas' version of the classic Greek pies made with fila pastry. They come with a great variety of fillings; mixed cheeses and egg, or spinach, egg and cheese (very similar to those used in the 'mezze' section) and meat or poultry, with or without vegetables, usually bound with a highly seasoned white sauce.

1 Choose a pan large enough to hold the leeks and the chicken. Wash and finely slice the leeks and cook them gently with a walnut-sized knob of butter until tender, about 20 minutes. Add the jointed chicken and boiling water to cover it by about 3 cm [1 in.]. Add salt and pepper and simmer gently for another 1 hour or so, until the chicken is very tender.

2 Take the pieces out of the pan with a slotted spoon, leaving the liquid in the pan. Skin and bone them and cut the meat into small pieces. Return them to the pan and boil quickly to reduce the cooking liquid to a very thick consistency. Allow to cool while you make a Béchamel Sauce with the flour, about 120 g [4 oz] of the butter and the milk. Add this and the grated cheese to the pan. Lightly beat and stir in the eggs and a little nutmeg; mix thoroughly.

3 Preheat the oven to moderate, 180°C [350°F, gas 4]. Melt the rest of the butter and use some of it to grease a medium rectangular ovenproof dish. Cover the bottom with half of the fila pastry sheets, lightly brushing each one with butter before setting the next one on top (see pages 10, 35 and 130). Spread on the filling and cover with the other sheets, again brushing each one with butter and finishing by brushing the top with the last of the butter. Score the surface into squares with a razor blade. Sprinkle the pie with a little water to keep the leaves from lifting (I find a plant spray ideal for this), and bake for 1 hour or until golden.

* This dish should be cooked in advance to this stage.

4 Let the pie cool completely, then slice it without taking it out of the dish. Reheat and serve warm.

CHICKEN KISHK

PREPARATION TIME
1½ hours, including 1 hour cooking

1 medium chicken, about 1.5 kg [3 lb]
3–4 medium onions
2 sticks celery
1 carrot
salt and pepper to taste
5–6 cracked cardamom pods
2.5 ml [½ tsp] crushed mastic (optional)
45 ml [3 tbsp] flour
45 ml [3 tbsp] natural yoghurt
15–30 ml [1–2 tbsp] clarified butter

(picture on page 62)

This is such a great favourite in Egypt that the name has become a term of endearment: you say that someone is 'a real kishk chicken'. Pieces of chicken are served with rice and a very thick, sharp-tasting yoghurt sauce enriched with onions browned in clarified butter. The sauce is a modern urban adaptation of the traditional 'kishk' made in the country. It is always served with rice. It isn't a dish for those who have to count their calories. Although it is such a well-known dish, I only learnt it a few years ago through a friend in London. Probably I had missed it when I was a child because of my aversion to soft-boiled food. Traditional 'Kishk' is quite different; wheat is boiled in sour milk, then dried in the sun and crushed. Sometimes, while still damp it is forced into small balls or sticks. It is then used to enrich and thicken soups and children often carry pieces in their pockets to crunch as one might eat sweets.

1 Cover the chicken in water and simmer for about 1 hour with one of the onions, the celery sticks, carrot, salt, pepper, cracked cardamom pods and crushed mastic (if available). When it is done, remove it from the pan, reserving the stock. Skin it, take the meat off the bone, cut it into large pieces and set aside. Return the rest of the carcase to the pan and continue simmering until the broth is full of flavour.

2 Make the sauce by stirring together the flour and yoghurt over a low heat and adding 4 or 5 ladlefuls of the hot stock, one at a time. When the taste of raw flour is gone and the sauce is cooked, reduce it to a very thick consistency. Set aside. Chop the rest of the onions, fry in clarified butter until brown and add, with the butter, to the sauce.

3 To serve, arrange the chicken pieces on top of a mound of rice and smother with sauce. This dish can be eaten either hot or cold; if hot, it may be advisable to reheat the chicken pieces briefly in the sauce.

Steamed Stuffed Chicken and Greek Chicken Pie

FRIED CHICKEN WITH SESAME SEEDS

PREPARATION TIME
**30 minutes, including 20
minutes cooking**

4 chicken pieces
1 egg
60 ml [4 tbsp] flour
2.5 ml [½ tsp] baking powder
salt and pepper to taste
170 g [6 oz] sesame seeds
oil for shallow frying

*This recipe was given to me by Jacqueline Biancardi, a superb cook, who also comes from
Egypt. She has travelled extensively, and this is reflected in her cooking. The following dish is
similar to the classic American 'Chicken Maryland', using sesame seeds instead of sweetcorn
to give it a Middle Eastern touch.*

1 Skin the chicken. Beat the egg and mix in the flour and baking powder to make a
thick, gluey batter. Dry the chicken pieces, sprinkle them with salt and pepper, dip in the
batter and roll in sesame seeds.

2 Heat the oil in a large, heavy-based frying pan. Add the chicken pieces and gently
shallow fry for about 10 minutes on each side, then drain on kitchen paper.

Left to right Chicken Kishk, Sfereya and Fried Chicken with Sesame Seeds, served on a bed of watercress

SFEREYA

This recipe for Sfereya, an Algerian dish, was given to me by my friend Dalila. It is garnished with roasted almonds and served with cheese and bread rissoles.

PREPARATION TIME
8 hours soaking
1 hour 20 minutes, including 1 hour cooking

100 g [3½ oz] chickpeas
6 chicken thighs
25 ml [1 heaped tbsp] clarified butter, or half oil, half butter
5 ml [1 tsp] ground cinnamon
1 egg yolk

RISSOLES

50 g [2 oz] soft breadcrumbs
50 g [2 oz] grated Cheddar
2.5 ml [½ tsp] baking powder
salt and pepper to taste
5 ml [1 tsp] ground cinnamon
1 egg
oil for shallow frying

TO SERVE

25 g [1 oz] blanched almonds

1 Put the chickpeas in a bowl, cover with water and leave to soak for at least 8 hours.
2 Sauté the chicken pieces in clarified butter (or oil and butter) in a heavy-based frying pan until golden brown on both sides. Add the ground cinnamon, salt and pepper to taste. Add the chickpeas and just enough water to cover, bring to the boil, turn down the heat and simmer for about 45 minutes while you prepare the rissoles and the almonds. If the chicken is tender before the chickpeas are cooked, remove it and keep warm.
3 Make the rissoles. Mix the breadcrumbs in a bowl with the grated cheese, baking powder, salt, pepper and cinnamon. Gradually beat the egg into the mixture. It must not be wet: you may not need all the egg. Mould the mixture into walnut-sized lumps. Shallow fry in oil until golden brown all over and keep warm. Gently roast the almonds under the grill or in a dry non-stick pan until lightly coloured.
4 Remove the chicken pieces from the pan and place them on a serving dish. Keep warm.
5 Thicken the sauce. Beat an egg yolk lightly in a cup, then beat in a little of the hot sauce, pour this mixture into a pan and heat gently, stirring. Taste, and adjust the seasoning. Pour the sauce over the chicken and scatter the roasted almonds over the top. Arrange the rissoles around it.

62

PERSIAN CHICKEN WITH RICE

PREPARATION TIME
**1 hour 45 minutes, including
    cooking**

CHICKEN
8 chicken thighs
1 small stick celery
1 small carrot
1 small onion
2 cloves garlic
**2–3 strands saffron (or a pinch
    turmeric)**
salt and pepper to taste

CARROTS IN CARAMEL
500 g [1 lb] medium carrots
30 g [1 oz] butter
salt and pepper to taste
1 large orange
30 ml [2 tbsp] sugar
15 ml [1 tbsp] water

**230 g [8 oz] Patna or basmati
    rice**
oil for mould

TO SERVE
**60 g [2 oz] whole peeled
    almonds**

(picture on page 64)

This dish of chicken with carrots, candied orange peel and rice is one of my students' favourites. All the separate elements can be prepared in advance. I like to make it with chicken thighs, which give neat, even pieces of meat. It can, of course, also be made with a whole jointed chicken.

1 Skin the chicken thighs. Chop the celery, carrot and onion into large chunks. Put in a saucepan with the garlic, saffron, salt and pepper, barely cover with water and poach for about 20 to 30 minutes or until the chicken is tender. Leave the chicken to cool in the stock so that it does not dry out.

2 Scrub the carrots and cut into matchsticks. Put them in a heavy-based pan with the butter, salt and pepper, and about a tablespoon of stock from the chicken. Bring to the boil, then lower the heat and simmer, covered, for about 10 minutes or until cooked, shaking the pan from time to time. When cooked, set aside.

3 Wash and scrub the orange, and peel it with a very sharp knife. Pare most of the pith off the peel and cut it into very thin strips. Blanch them in boiling water for a couple of minutes, then drain.

4 Make a caramel syrup by boiling the sugar with a little water in a small pan until it turns a pale golden colour. Add the blanched orange strips and continue cooking until the caramel becomes slightly more coloured. Pour over the carrots and mix in.

5 Cook the rice in the Persian style (see page 106). Preheat the oven to moderate, 180°C [350°F, gas 4]. Oil a large ring mould and arrange the pieces of chicken in it with some of the carrots in little clumps between. Fill the mould with rice, packing it in firmly so that there are no gaps. (If you have managed to form a crust in the rice pan, reserve this – uncovered.)

6 Heat the moulded chicken and rice in the oven for a few minutes (even if nothing has been left to cool). Add a little stock to the carrots and caramel and reheat. Reduce the rest of the stock to make a thick sauce. Gently dry roast the almonds.

7 Turn the mould out on to a serving dish and fill the centre with the caramelized carrots and orange peel. Pour some of the stock over it to colour it and sprinkle with chopped roasted almonds. If you have the rice crust, cut it in into triangles and set them around the edge of the dish. Serve the sauce separately.

If you prefer, simply pile the chicken pieces on to the rice and pour the sauce over it.

Middle Eastern cooking makes surprisingly exotic use of familiar ingredients, as with the caramelized carrots in this Iranian chicken dish (above). RIGHT Huge piles of carrots, white turnips and pumpkins, with the green tops sold separately, at a Berber market in Morocco.

Two festive poultry dishes: Persian Chicken with Rice and Pastilla

PASTILLA

PREPARATION TIME
3 hours 10 minutes, including cooking

SERVES 10–12

30 ml [2 tbsp] **oil**
750 g [1½ lb] **onions**
1 clove garlic
salt and pepper to taste
6–8 strands saffron (or 5 ml [1 tsp] **turmeric)**
8 ml [1 heaped tsp] **ground ginger**
20 ml [4 tsp] **ground cinnamon**
1 medium chicken, about 1.5 kg [3 lb]
a good teacupful very finely chopped parsley
250 g [8 oz] **peeled almonds**
30–45 ml [2–3 tbsp] **sugar**
juice of ½ lemon
7–8 size 2 [large] **eggs**
30 g [1 oz] **butter**
450 g [1 lb] **fila pastry**

TO SERVE

15–20 ml [3–4 tsp] **icing sugar**
15–20 ml [3–4 tsp] **ground cinnamon**

This is a famous Moroccan festive dish, usually made with pigeons. It takes a long time to prepare, and is quite complicated, though not actually difficult. However, it is spectacular and well worth the time and effort. This version was shown to me by Fatima Ma'toughi.

If making this dish for the first time, I advise you to prepare the two fillings in advance. For general advice on handling fila pastry, see page 130.

1 Choose a saucepan or flameproof casserole that will comfortably take the jointed chicken and the onions: they should not more than half fill it, so that it is easy to turn them. Pour in oil to a depth of about 3 cm [1 in.] and set over medium heat. Grate the onions and add, stirring from time to time. Thinly slice the garlic and add with the salt and pepper, saffron (or turmeric), ginger, and a teaspoonful of the cinnamon. Joint the chicken and add the pieces to the pan. Raise the heat a little and cook for about 1 hour, turning the pieces from time to time.

2 Add the chopped parsley. Cook for another 30 minutes or until the meat comes off the bones easily.

3 Dry roast the almonds, grind them roughly and mix with 2 or 3 tablespoonfuls of sugar and the rest of the cinnamon. Set aside.

4 When the chicken is cooked, remove the pieces with a slotted spoon and set aside to cool. Strain the contents of the pan into a bowl. Reserve the stock and put the parsley and onions back in the pan. Add the lemon juice, then break 6 or 7 of the eggs into the pan. Stir gently until they begin to set. The whole mixture should have the texture of a purée. Set it aside while you skin and bone the chicken and cut into bite-sized pieces.

5 Melt the butter and use some of it to grease your largest roasting pan. Put a sheet of fila pastry lengthways in the centre, moisten it lightly all over with fingers dipped in the reserved chicken stock, and set a second sheet of fila the same size on top. Follow the step-by-step instructions opposite. (Moisten each sheet of fila in this way to stop them from sticking together.) Arrange more sheets of fila radiating outwards like the petals of

a flower, with the inner end of each resting on the first two sheets and the outer end hanging over the edge of the roasting pan. Overlap the sheets until they are about 4 layers thick all round.

6 Pile the chicken pieces on the fila in a tidy rectangle the same size as the first 2 sheets. Spread the parsley mixture on top. Cover with 1 sheet of fila. One by one, lift up the outer ends of the top layer of the overlapping fila sheets, fold each one over the rectangle and stick each one lightly in place by moistening it with your hands dipped into beaten egg. Take care to keep the rectangle compact.

7 Add most of the rest of the melted butter to the almond mixture and check the balance of the flavours: the almond, cinnamon and sugar should each be distinct, without overwhelming the others. Correct the proportions if necessary. Spread this mixture on top of the now nearly completed pie and smooth it gently with your fingers. Place 2 more layers of fila on top, lengthways, exactly like the first 2 layers. Fold over and stick down the remaining outer sheets of fila as in step 6. Check that the filling is evenly protected by the pastry all round. To complete the packet, place more sheets of fila crossways over it and tuck underneath. Preheat the oven to $180°C$ [$350°F$, gas 4].

8 Brush the pastilla with melted butter and bake it for about 30 minutes or until golden brown. Let it cool a little, then decorate with trails of icing sugar and ground cinnamon.

PASTILLA

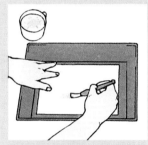

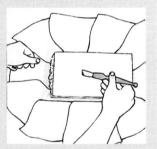

1 Lay a rectangular sheet of fila in a large roasting pan. (The rectangle should be a little smaller than the base of the pan.) Brush the pastry with chicken stock, and lay another sheet of fila the same size on top to form the base.

2 Arrange more sheets of fila in the pan so that they overlap like the petals of a flower, making sure the base is covered. Brush each sheet with stock as you go along. Add more overlapping sheets until they are about 4 layers thick all round.

3 Pile the chicken mixture on to the pastry, then spread on the parsley mixture. Cover with a rectangle of fila the same size as the base, and brush it with stock.

4 One by one, fold the top layer of the overlapping sheets of fila into the centre of the rectangle and stick each one lightly in place by moistening it with beaten egg. Spread the almond mixture on top, then a double layer of rectangles of fila the same size as the base. Fold over and stick down the remaining overlapping sheets of fila as before.

5 Lay two or three rectangles of fila crossways over the packet.

6 Tuck the edges of the crossways sheets underneath the packet, which should be neat, completely enclosing the filling.

EGG DISHES

Eggah is a general term for a wide variety of egg dishes similar to Spanish omelettes, found all over the Middle East. However, the name varies from country to country: *eggah* is the Egyptian word, while in Tunisia it is *tajine* and in Iran *kuku*. (I have used the names arbitrarily.) The consistency varies according to how many eggs are used. With a large number of eggs it has a light texture, almost like a soufflé; using fewer eggs makes it more solid.

The beauty of *eggah* is their versatility. Any of them can be served cold, cut into small cubes, as *mezze*; or hot or cold as hors d'oeuvres; or as a light lunch dish with a salad. They are ideal for picnics. The quantities given here are for a light lunch for four; as *mezze* they would serve six or eight people.

Cooking times for *eggah* are variable, and you can choose the cooking method according to the time you have. In a frying pan an *eggah* takes only about 10 minutes; in a moderate oven, 180°C [350°F, gas 4], it takes up to 45 minutes. The cooking time also depends on the thickness of the *eggah*. Ideally, aim for a depth of 3 cm [1 in.] when the mixture is poured into the pan. If baking, put the filled baking dish on a preheated baking sheet, as you would a quiche, to avoid the centre or bottom remaining undercooked or soggy. Test by touching the surface with your finger to see if it is firm.

Eggah sometimes have a tendency to become springy or rubbery in texture on cooling. I believe that this is due to air bubbles, created by beating the eggs, forming a kind of foam cushion. For this reason I recommend that the eggs are stirred in gently with a palette knife or a spoon, whether the dish is to be eaten hot or cold. You will find *eggah* recipes in the vegetable chapter: one with spinach and another with leeks (pages 96–7). Another favourite is made with sautéed and well-spiced minced meat to which you add raw spring onion, uncooked tomatoes cut into very small cubes and lots of chopped parsley.

HERB KUKU

This dish, made with fresh herbs, must be eaten cold. If you taste a piece hot, and another cold, you will see how the blend of gentle flavours has developed.

Mix 45 ml [3 tbsp] chopped parsley with 30 ml [2 tbsp] each chopped coriander and mint. Add 45 ml [3 tbsp] each coarsely chopped walnuts and whole raisins. Stir in 5 or 6 size 2 (large) eggs one by one. Add salt and pepper to taste and 5 ml [1 tsp] each ground allspice and crushed dill weed. Stir gently, taste and adjust the seasoning. Transfer the mixture to a greased ovenproof dish and bake in the oven, preheated to 180°C [350°F, gas 4] for 30–40 minutes, or cook gently in a frying pan in a little oil and butter for about 10 minutes (see page 97).

TUNISIAN TAJINE

Heat 15 ml [1 tbsp] oil in a heavy-based pan over a low heat. Add 200 g [7 oz] lean minced lamb, 150 g [5 oz] chopped lamb's liver and salt and pepper to taste. Cook gently, stirring, until the meat is brown. Stir in 60 g [2 oz] chopped parsley, 15 ml [1 tbsp] dried breadcrumbs and 60 g [2 oz] grated Cheddar or similar cheese into the pan and mix well. Stir in 6 size 2 (large) eggs one by one. Taste and adjust the seasoning. Transfer the mixture to a greased deep ovenproof dish. The mixture should be 5–7 cm [2–3 in.] deep. Bake in the oven, preheated to 180°C [350°F, gas 4] for about 25 minutes until the top centre is firm to the touch.

Front Spinach Eggah, Leek and Potato Eggah (*recipes on pages 96–7*) and Tunisian Tajine, *Back* Herb Kuku and Cabbage Salad (*recipe on page 25*)

MEAT

The meats most closely associated with Middle Eastern cooking are mutton and lamb, but veal and beef are also widely available. Pork is popular in Greece and Cyprus, but since both Moslem and Jewish dietary law forbid it, it is little used elsewhere. With few exceptions, recipes of the region usually call for 'meat', without specifying either the kind or the cut, and in most of the recipes in this chapter it is in fact possible to substitute other meats for those specified.

The many ways of cooking meat include grilling for tender cuts, baking and stewing with vegetables and pulses, and braising with sauces flavoured with spices and herbs and enriched with dried fruits and nuts. Minced meat of all kinds, which is much used throughout the Middle East, is often made into meatballs, which may be grilled, fried or braised in delicious sauces.

Middle Eastern cooks excel in the art of cooking stews, blending different ingredients according to what is available and what they can afford, but most of all relying on the inspiration of the moment. A *tajine* is simply a stew cooked in a North African dish with a spectacular pointed lid, rather like a hat, which is very suitable for slow cooking on hot ashes.

Middle Eastern meat dishes usually include vegetables, dried fruit or grains in varying proportions: sometimes the meat is the main ingredient and in other recipes it is the flavouring. *Top left* Baked Leg of Lamb with Okra, *below left* Shoulder of Lamb Stuffed with Apricots and *right* Lamb with Pasta

69

BAKED LAMB

Lamb baked on its own or with vegetables or pasta is a great favourite in the Middle East. When there is no oven at home, or when the oven is not large enough, the meat is still often sent to the local baker, with very precise cooking instructions.

LEG OF LAMB WITH OKRA

PREPARATION TIME
2½ hours, including 20 minutes cooking

½ leg of lamb
a little oil + oil for shallow frying
salt and pepper to taste
5–6 cloves garlic
1 large onion
4–5 tomatoes
15 ml [1 tbsp] tomato purée
1 teacupful hot water
500 g [1 lb] okra
½ teacupful vinegar
15 ml [1 tbsp] ground coriander seed
juice of 1 lemon

(picture on page 68)

Fresh okra is now quite widely available; Middle Eastern greengrocers have it under the name of 'bamia' and Indian ones call it 'bhindi'. The smaller and younger it is, the better – choose fresh, young pods wherever possible. See page 87 for tips on preparation.

1 Preheat the oven to hot, 220°C [425°F, gas 7]. Trim excess fat from the meat with a sharp knife. Rub it with a little oil, salt and pepper. Cut 2 of the cloves of garlic into slivers and insert into small cuts in the meat. Put the meat in the oven while you prepare the sauce.

2 Grate the onion, and skin and chop the tomatoes. Dilute the tomato purée in a teacupful of hot water, add salt and pepper and mix with the tomatoes and onion. Spoon the tomato and onion mixture over the meat and turn it over once or twice to coat it. Return to the oven, lower the heat to moderate, 180°C [350°F, gas 4], and cook for about 2 hours or until the meat is done to your taste – though for this kind of dish it is best to have the meat well cooked rather than underdone in the French way.

3 Wash the okra and peel the tops. Soak in vinegar and water for about 30 minutes.

4 Rinse and dry the okra well. Crush 3 or 4 cloves of garlic and set aside. Pour oil into a deep fryer to a depth of about 3 cm [at least 1 in.] and heat it until quite hot. Fry a few okra at a time until golden. (Be careful, since the oil tends to splutter. The fryer, used with its basket, keeps the problem to a minimum.) Use a slotted spoon to transfer the okra to a sieve for a couple of minutes to shed oil. Sprinkle with salt and finish draining on kitchen paper. Take the oil off the heat.

5 When the meat is cooked, take it out of the oven and keep warm. Put the okra into the roasting pan. Make a Ta'leya. Pour away most of the oil, leaving about a tablespoonful. Lightly fry the garlic and ground coriander, add a little of the juice from the roast meat, stir and tip the mixture over the okra. Add the lemon juice and mix gently with a large metal spoon. Taste and adjust the seasoning.

6 Clear a space in the centre of the dish, put back the meat and return to the oven for at least another 20 minutes, or until the okra is cooked. (It doesn't matter if some of the okra is a bit squashed.) This dish is delicious with rice, or just bread and a green salad.

The whole dish can also be cooked on top of the stove. The meat is browned in a heavy-based pan or casserole, to which the fried okra is added when the meat is tender.

Sides of lamb hanging in the window of a traditionally tiled butcher's shop in Cairo. Lamb – and mutton – is the only meat eaten by the enormous majority of people in the Middle East: pork is forbidden by Moslem religious law and beef is only for the wealthy. The fattiest cuts of lamb are the most highly prized.

BAKED SHOULDER OF LAMB STUFFED WITH APRICOTS

PREPARATION TIME
3–4 hours soaking
2 hours 20–40 minutes,
    including 2–2½ hours
    cooking and 30 minutes
    soaking

120 g [4 oz] dried apricots
1 small onion
salt and pepper to taste
1 shoulder of lamb (with or
    without the bone)
5 ml [1 tsp] coriander seed
a little olive oil

(picture on page 68)

Lamb goes extremely well with dried fruits such as prunes, quinces and apricots. Ask your butcher to cut a hollow pocket in the shoulder to contain the stuffing, or do it yourself by whichever method you know best. You should also remove as much fat as possible from the shoulder, or ask the butcher to do so.

1 Cover the apricots with water and soak for 3 to 4 hours.
2 Chop the apricots and the onion very finely, add salt and pepper and mix well. This can be done in a food processor: chop rather than purée it. Reserve the water.
3 Preheat the oven to hot, 230°C [450°F, gas 8]. Prepare and trim the shoulder if necessary. Gently dry roast and coarsely crush the coriander seed. Oil your hands and use them to rub salt, pepper, coriander and oil into the outside of the lamb. Spoon the apricot mixture into the pocket, pushing it as far in as you can, and secure with skewers if necessary. Put the meat in an ovenproof dish: it should just fit the dish. If any stuffing is left over, put it around the meat. Add a teacupful of the soaking water, and put the meat in the oven. Roast it for about 30 minutes, turning it over after about 15 minutes. Then lower the heat to warm, 160° [325°F, gas 3], and cook for another 1½ to 2 hours, depending on size. After the first hour check that the liquid is not drying up and if necessary add a little hot water. In any case scrape around the dish to that the juice gets mixed with the sticky bits and stuffing, and spoon over the shoulder. Serve with rice, couscous or Pourgouri Pilafi (see page 107).

I often mix the apricots with prunes and sometimes add a handful of coarsely chopped walnuts.

You can, of course, use this kind of stuffing for a more traditional European boned shoulder of lamb. A small leg of lamb or even chump chops can be given the same exotic flavour if they are surrounded by the fruit and pot-roasted.

LAMB WITH PASTA

PREPARATION TIME
1 hour 40 minutes, including
    1½ hours cooking

1 kg [or 2¼ lb] lean lamb, either
    fillet or cut from the leg or
    shoulder
salt and pepper to taste
juice of ½–1 lemon
30 ml [2 tbsp] olive oil
1 small onion
5 ml [1 tsp] crushed dried
    rigani (or oregano)
200 ml [7 fl oz] dry white wine
10 ml [2 tsp] tomato purée
1 teacupful boiling water
400 g [14 oz] orzo (small pasta
    grains; see page 109)
150 g [5 oz] grated Parmesan

(picture on page 69)

The recipe for this dish, known in Greek as 'arni youvetsi', is from Jacqueline Biancardi. 'Rigani', a type of oregano which grows in Greece, is normally used to flavour the meat. Ordinary oregano is a perfectly adequate substitute.

1 Preheat the oven to hot, 220°C [425°F, gas 7]. Trim the meat and cut it into 5 cm [2 in.] chunks. Put it in a medium-sized ovenproof dish, season with salt and pepper, and add the lemon juice and oil. Toss well to coat the meat and put it in the oven for 10 to 15 minutes to brown, turning it over once.
2 Chop the onion, add to the meat with the *rigani* (or oregano) and pour over the wine. Reduce the heat to warm, 160°C [325°F, gas 3], and cook for another 40 minutes.
3 Remove the meat with a slotted spoon and set aside. Dilute the tomato purée in a teacupful of boiling water and pour into the dish, then add the pasta and mix well. The pasta should be just covered with liquid: add more boiling water if necessary. Taste, and adjust the seasoning. Return the dish to the oven for about another 30 minutes. Put the meat back in the dish and return to the oven for 15 minutes to reheat. Serve sprinkled with grated Parmesan.

If you want to use larger short pasta, such as shells or bows, parboil it before adding it to the sauce.

In our family we used to make this dish differently. The meat and onions were browned and cooked (without tomatoes) in a heavy-based saucepan on top of the stove, and the pasta browned separately by quick shallow frying in hot oil before being transferred to the saucepan to finish cooking with the meat and its juices.

Spiced Crown of Lamb, served with game chips

SPICED CROWN OF LAMB

PREPARATION TIME
1 hour 40 minutes, including
  1½ hours cooking

1 crown of lamb with 14 chops
5 ml [1 tsp] ground ginger
2–3 strands saffron or 5 ml [1 tsp] turmeric
5 ml [1 tsp] ground cumin seed
salt and pepper to taste
30 ml [2 tbsp] oil
about 10 small onions
15 ml [1 tbsp] water

This is a good example of a typically British dish that can be transformed and given a Middle Eastern flavour simply by altering the seasoning. It is an anglicized adaptation of a dish cooked for me by my Moroccan friend Fatima Ma'toughi. She makes it with loin of lamb and serves it with fried chipped potatoes (see below).

1 Preheat the oven to 180°C [350°F, gas 4]. Mix all the seasoning ingredients with a tablespoonful of the oil. Reserve a teaspoonful of the spice mixture and rub the rest into the meat. Put the meat in a baking dish and cook in the oven for about 1½ hours, or until the meat is tender.
2 Cook the onions separately in the rest of the oil and a tablespoonful of water with the rest of the spice mixture. Put them into the centre of the crown and roast for another 10 minutes.
3 Serve with game chips.

LOIN OF LAMB WITH CHIPPED POTATOES Rub a loin of lamb with the spice mixture described here and put in a flameproof casserole with 2 teacupfuls of water. Bring to the boil over a medium heat. Add the onions, reduce the heat and simmer, covered, for about 30 minutes, or until the onions are cooked. Transfer the meat and onions to an ovenproof casserole and brown in a hot oven, 220°C [425°F, gas 7] for 15 to 20 minutes.

TUNISIAN KAMOUNIYA

PREPARATION TIME
1 hour, including 40 minutes
    cooking

30 ml [2 tbsp] olive oil
1 large onion
200 g [8 oz] each lamb's heart,
    kidneys and liver
10 ml [2 tsp] ground cumin
    seed
salt to taste
6 tomatoes
10 ml [2 tsp] tomato purée
2.5 ml [½ tsp] harissa or other
    red chilli sauce
10 ml [2 tsp] turmeric

(picture on page 74)

Kamouniya means 'with Kamoun' – 'with cumin' in Arabic. This delicious offal recipe was given to me by a Tunisian friend. There is also an Egyptian dish called 'kamouneya', made with stewing lamb or beef and cooked in a similar way.

1 Put the oil into a heavy-based pan. Finely chop the onion and cook gently until soft and transparent.
2 Cut the heart and kidneys in half and carefully remove the skin and membranes. Cut the meat into cubes and add to the pan with half the ground cumin seed. Brown gently for a few minutes. Add enough water to just cover the meat, add salt and bring to the boil, then simmer, covered, for about 30 minutes.
3 Cut the liver into cubes, skin and deseed the tomatoes and add to the pan with the tomato purée, harissa and turmeric. Bring back to the boil and simmer for a further 10 minutes.
4 Mix the rest of the cumin with a little water. Just before serving, tip this into the mixture, stir well and adjust the salt to taste.

HIGADO CON VINAGRE

PREPARATION TIME
40–50 minutes, including 15
    minutes cooking

750 g [1½ lb] lamb's liver
fine dried breadcrumbs for
    coating + 15 ml [1 tbsp]
2 cloves garlic
oil for shallow frying
15 ml [1 tbsp] tomato purée
30 ml [2 tbsp] vinegar
½ teacupful water
salt and pepper to taste

(picture on page 74)

The names of most Sephardic Jewish dishes, like the Sephardis themselves, have come from mediaeval Spain: Higado con vinagre simply means 'liver with vinegar' in Spanish. This is how my grandmother always cooked liver. Generally, lamb's liver would be used, although I like it best with calf's liver, for which I have given instructions below.

1 Trim and slice the liver. Coat the slices with fine dried breadcrumbs. Finely chop the garlic.
2 Choose a frying pan into which all the slices will fit easily, and pour in oil to a depth of about 1 cm [⅜ in.]. Heat the oil until it sizzles and put in the slices. Cook for a few seconds on each side to brown. Remove them and drain on kitchen paper.
3 Carefully pour away most of the oil. Return the pan to the heat and quickly fry the garlic and remaining tablespoonful of breadcrumbs. Add the tomato purée. As soon as the mixture starts sticking, pour in the vinegar and half a teacupful of water, and stir. Return the liver to the pan. Add salt and pepper to taste. Turn the slices over so that they are evenly coated with the sauce. Half cover the pan and simmer for about 5 or 10 minutes. If the sauce starts to dry out too quickly, add a little water.
4 When the liver is cooked, transfer it to a serving dish and keep warm. Taste the sauce and adjust the seasoning if necessary. If it is too liquid, reduce it; it should be rather thick. Pour the sauce over the liver and serve hot.

If you use calf's liver, which needs only a few minutes' cooking, don't fry it before the sauce is cooked. Prepare the sauce first by frying the garlic and a tablespoon of breadcrumbs, then adding the tomato purée, vinegar and water. Simmer the sauce for about 10 to 15 minutes. Quickly brown the liver slices in a little very hot oil in a separate frying pan – not more than a minute each side, then transfer to the sauce and simmer for a couple of minutes.

BREADCRUMBS
Leftover bread will dry in a few days uncovered in the refrigerator. I do not generally discard the crust, but while the bread is still soft I cut it into small pieces which can then easily be ground in a pestle and mortar, or food processor, then pushed through a sieve.

Soft breadcrumbs Traditionally, soft breadcrumbs are made from stale bread without crusts which is soaked in stock, milk·or water, pressed to remove excess moisture, then crumbled. However, if you do this with modern mass-produced bread, the result is rather like wallpaper paste. So let it go slightly stale, but then do not soak it. Pass it through a mincer with a fine disc or a rotary cheese grater, or use a food processor.

LAMB, FENNEL AND BROAD BEAN TAJINE

This is another dish cooked for me by my Moroccan friend, Fatima Ma'toughi.

PREPARATION TIME
1 hour 20 minutes, including
    50 minutes–1 hour 10
    minutes cooking

30 ml [2 tbsp] oil
1 medium onion
½ lemon
450–700 g [1–1½ lb] stewing
    lamb
salt and pepper to taste
5 ml [1 tsp] ground ginger
3–4 tomatoes
2 medium heads fennel
700 g [1½ lb] fresh, or 250 g [or
    ½ lb] frozen broad beans
45 ml [3 tbsp] chopped fresh
    coriander
1 teacupful water

1 Choose a flameproof casserole large enough for all the ingredients to only half fill it. Pour in enough oil to coat the base of the pan, set it over medium heat and grate in the onion. Wash and scrub the lemon, cut into slices and add.
2 Cut the lamb into 5 cm [2 in.] cubes and add them to the casserole with salt, pepper and ginger. Cook on medium heat, half covered, turning the meat occasionally, for 15 minutes. Skin and chop the tomatoes and add to the casserole. Cook for another 15 minutes, or until the meat is tender.
3 Meanwhile wash the fennel heads, discarding any brown or withered parts. Cut each one into large chunks. Pod the broad beans if fresh; if frozen, leave unthawed. When the meat is tender add the fennel, beans and chopped coriander. Add a teacupful of water or, if using frozen broad beans, half a teacupful. Bring back to the boil, lower the heat and simmer until the vegetables are cooked, about 10 minutes. Taste, adjust the seasoning and serve with rice, couscous or Pourgouri Pilafi (see page 107). Don't remove the slices of lemon: they should be tender and delicious.

Artichokes also go well with broad beans. For convenience, add canned artichoke hearts once the broad beans are cooked.

LAMB WITH PRUNES AND APRICOTS

PREPARATION TIME
3–4 hours soaking
1 hour 35 minutes, including 1
  hour 10 minutes cooking

120 g [4 oz] stoned prunes
120 g [4 oz] dried apricots
30 ml [2 tbsp] oil
1 medium onion
750 g [or 1½ lb] lamb fillet or
  cut from the leg or shoulder
5 ml [1 tsp] ground allspice
salt and pepper to taste
15 ml [1 tbsp] sesame seeds
1 recipe Plain Pilaf Rice
  (see page 104)

1 Rinse the prunes and dried apricots, cover with water and soak for 3 or 4 hours.
2 Pour enough oil into a heavy-based saucepan to coat the bottom thinly. Grate the onion into it and set over medium heat. Cut the meat into 5 cm [2 in.] chunks and add it to the pan. Add the allspice, salt and pepper, and mix well. Half cover the pan and cook for about 30 minutes, turning from time to time. If the meat sticks, scrape the pan and add a little of the soaking liquid from the fruit.
3 When the meat is nearly cooked, add the fruit and enough soaking liquid to just cover it, bring back to the boil and reduce the heat to simmer. Cook for another 30 minutes or until the liquid has thickened. Meanwhile, gently roast the sesame seeds in a dry frying pan and prepare the Pilaf Rice.
4 To serve, use an oiled mould to form a ring of rice, and turn it out on the serving dish. Spoon the meat and fruit in and around the ring; sprinkle with roasted sesame seeds.

This dish is also delicious cooked with only one of the two fruits, or with pork instead of lamb. A more exotic ingredient to cook with lamb in this way is fresh quinces. A tablespoonful of ground almonds mixed into the sauce makes a rich alternative.

Left to right Lamb, Fennel and Broad Bean Tajine, Lamb with Prunes and Apricots, Tunisian Kamouniya and Higado con Vinagre

Pork Afelia may be served with rice or Pourgouri Pilafi (*recipe on page 107*)

PORK AFELIA

PREPARATION TIME
Marinating time 2 hours
$1\frac{1}{4}$ hours, including cooking

500 g [1 lb] pork, either fillet,
** or cut from the leg or**
** shoulder**
about 175 ml [6 fl oz] red wine
30 ml [2 tbsp] olive oil
10 ml [2 tsp] coarsely crushed
** coriander seed**
salt to taste

1 Trim the pork and cut it into chunks. Put them in a bowl, cover with red wine and leave to marinate for at least 2 hours.

2 Remove the meat from the marinade with a slotted spoon, reserving the marinade. Dry it with kitchen paper. Brown the meat in olive oil in a heavy-based saucepan, in batches if necessary. Pour out most of the oil, leaving just enough to gently fry the coriander seed until the fragrance develops. Pour in the marinade, scrape the pan and return the meat. Add salt to taste.

3 Bring the liquid to the boil, turn down the heat and simmer, covered, for about 1 hour or until the meat is tender. When the meat is cooked, the liquid should be reduced and thick. If it is too thin, remove the meat temporarily and raise the heat to reduce the sauce.

This dish goes well with Pourgouri Pilafi (see page 107), or rice.

KOFTA

'Kofta' is Arabic for minced rissoles, which are either grilled, fried or cooked in sauces, or added to soups or vegetables.

The first time I introduce them to students I use a minimum of flavouring to show that if well prepared, kofta are delicious. But they must be thoroughly kneaded (see below) so that all the flavours blend in and the mixture is soft and even. Try this simple seasoning first, then ring the changes with different spices. I cannot overestimate the importance of kneading the meat until it is smoothly blended: this is the key to success for any 'kofta' recipe. Your hands will get sticky, but the illustrations at the bottom of the page will show you how to avoid it.

GRILLED LAMB KOFTA

PREPARATION TIME
20 minutes, including cooking (but depending on taste)

I small onion
500 g [I lb] minced lamb: fillet or cut from leg
salt and pepper to taste
30 ml [2 tbsp] chopped parsley
1.5 ml [¼ tsp] ground cumin seed

Ideally it is best to use an iron grid.

1 Grate the onion into the meat and add the other ingredients. Knead well (see below), taste and adjust the seasoning.
2 Heat the grid or grill. You can make kofta in different shapes: small fingers about 5 cm (1 in) long or flat rounds about 3–4 cm in diameter, not forgetting to knead well before shaping.
3 Place on the grid or under the grill. The kofta should seize immediately and by the time you have placed the last one on the grid, the first one will be ready to turn over.
4 When brown all over and still juicy inside, remove and serve on a bed of shredded lettuce, or in pitta bread with tahina and Egyptian Salad (see page 25).

If you shape the kofta like a hamburger you will find that even the most unadventurous children will like them.

You can vary the flavouring by adding any, or a combination, of the following: a grated clove of garlic, a touch of harissa or chilli powder or chopped coriander leaves. Or you can replace the cumin with ground caraway.

FORMING BALLS OR FINGER SHAPES

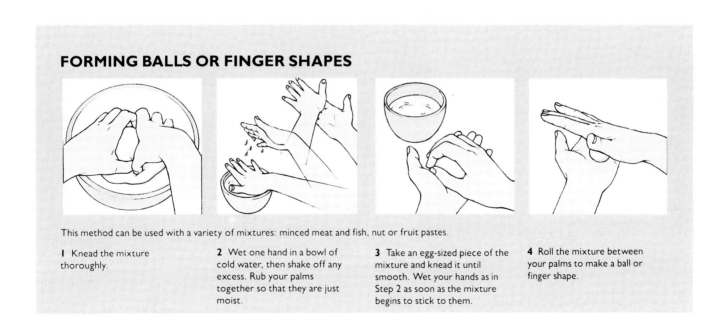

This method can be used with a variety of mixtures: minced meat and fish, nut or fruit pastes.

I Knead the mixture thoroughly.

2 Wet one hand in a bowl of cold water, then shake off any excess. Rub your palms together so that they are just moist.

3 Take an egg-sized piece of the mixture and knead it until smooth. Wet your hands as in Step 2 as soon as the mixture begins to stick to them.

4 Roll the mixture between your palms to make a ball or finger shape.

NOTE This tip on shaping minced meat also applies to minced or pounded chicken and fish mixtures (pages 39 and 52), to savoury pastes for rissoles (pages 18 and 110) and to pastries for biscuits and *petits fours* (pages 124, 125 and 128).

BARBECUES

Charcoal-grilled kebabs are the best known of all Middle Eastern dishes. Also popular for grilling are Kofta (minced meat rissoles; see the recipe on the previous page), small lamb chops, liver, poussins, quails and fish. They are served with various sauces, dips, pickles and condiments, and plenty of bread and salads. Their distinctively Middle Eastern character usually comes from marination in a simple mixture flavoured with grated onion, garlic, parsley, salt and pepper. Other spices and herbs are often added: some people use *rigani* (Greek oregano), others cumin, coriander, allspice or harissa.

As children our favourite treat was to be taken to a restaurant in Cairo which specialized in barbecuing. Ordering was done not by portion but by weight: a *ratl* (about 450 g or 1 lb) of kofta; another of kebab; and two of *risha* – this word means 'feather', and referred to the finest chops, cut from the best end and trimmed of all fat. While we waited, we were tantalized by the aroma of the meats

being cooked on a charcoal grill in full view, and our impatience was kept in check only by the constant arrival of *mezze*: pickles and tahina to eat with vast quantities of Arabic bread. From time to time we would call the waiters and threaten to cancel the order if they did not hurry, as we had already satisfied our hunger. But they knew that the moment the fragrant grilled meats arrived, lying on huge beds of parsley, we would change our minds and fall to with renewed appetite. The restaurant never put onions or pieces of pepper on the skewers, and I still dislike such additions myself.

KEBABS AND CUTLETS

Mix a finely grated medium onion with the same quantities of salt, pepper, cumin and parsley used in the Kofta recipe on the previous page. Spread this mixture over 500 g [1 lb] cubed lean lamb and 4 trimmed best end lamb cutlets. Leave in the refrigerator for at least 1 hour,

turning from time to time to make sure the mixture is evenly spread over the meat. Grill on the barbecue until the meat is done to your taste and serve on a bed of chopped fresh coriander leaves, sprigs of parsley or shredded lettuce.

Recipes for grilled fish and poussins, which are both also good barbecued, are on pages 46 and 58.

Kebabs, served on a bed of coriander leaves, eaten with a sprinkling of the red spice sumac, a dip such as Tahina, a mixture of pickles, bread and perhaps Tabbouleh (recipe on page 24), make a wonderful summer barbecue. On the barbecue above are quails, poussins, chicken breasts, large and small Kofta and chops. Pitta bread may be heated through for a few minutes on the grill when the meat is cooked and you are ready to eat

DRIED HERBS

When using dried herbs, always rub them between the palms of your hands before adding them to the dish. This releases the flavour and pulverizes the herb so that it blends in better. If the herb contains bits of twig, rub it through a wire-mesh tea strainer.

HERBS, SPICES AND SALT

If when tasting a dish to adjust the quantities of herbs and spices, you think it needs a bit more of everything, first try adding a little more salt. Taste again, and you will find that all the other flavours are enhanced.

MEAT BALLS (KOFTA) IN TOMATO SAUCE

PREPARATION TIME
1 hour, including 50 minutes
    cooking

30 ml [2 tbsp] oil + more for
    shallow frying
1 medium onion
salt and pepper to taste
5 ml [1 tsp] crushed dried
    limes, or juice of ½ lemon
1 400 g [14 oz] can tomatoes
15 ml [1 tbsp] tomato purée
30 g [1 oz] soft breadcrumbs
350 g [12 oz] minced beef or
    lamb, or a mixture of the two
a few sprigs fresh mint,
    chopped, or 5 ml [1 tsp]
    crushed dried mint
30 ml [2 tbsp] chopped parsley
5 ml [1 tsp] ground cumin seed

There is an infinite variety of meat ball dishes in the Middle East. In this recipe the meat balls are poached in a tomato sauce; it is also common to poach them in egg and lemon sauce.

1 Take a heavy-based saucepan and pour in just enough oil to cover the bottom. Set over medium heat. Grate the onion and add all but about a tablespoonful of it to the pan. Add salt, pepper and crushed dried limes or lemon juice. When the onion begins to brown, lower the heat. Drain the tomatoes and add to the pan with the tomato purée. Continue cooking, half covered.

2 Meanwhile, prepare the meat balls. Mix the breadcrumbs with the minced meat, the rest of the grated onion, salt, pepper, mint, chopped parsley and ground cumin. Knead well with dampened hands (see page 77), and form into walnut-sized balls: there should be enough for about 2 dozen meat balls.

3 Fry the meat balls in a little oil until brown and drain on kitchen paper. Tip them into the pan, shake well, taste and adjust the seasoning. Simmer, covered, for about 30 minutes. Serve with rice.

The tomato sauce can be flavoured in a variety of other ways: for example, with roasted crushed coriander seed, a little chilli sauce, turmeric and ginger. A handful of chopped parsley can be added to the sauce just before the tomatoes. The minced meat is often blended with cooked vegetables, such as leeks, aubergines or courgettes, very finely chopped, instead of breadcrumbs.

Chickpeas are one of the most characteristic ingredients of North African cuisine but pulses are a staple everywhere. BELOW Beans, lentils, seeds and nuts on sale in Nazareth market.

Meat balls in Tomato Sauce and Beef, Lamb, Chickpea and Egg Pie, served with a simple salad of tomatoes, cucumber and parsley

BEEF, LAMB, CHICKPEA AND EGG PIE

PREPARATION TIME
8 hours soaking
1½–2 hours, including 1–1¼ hours cooking if using a pressure cooker (add another 1 hour 40 minutes if not)

SERVES 8

80 g [3 oz] chickpeas
2 small onions
15 ml [1 tbsp] oil
750 g [or 1½ lb] shin of beef
pepper to taste
5 ml [1 tsp] ground cinnamon
salt to taste
250 g [or 8 oz] minced lamb
100 g [3½ oz] grated Cheddar, or other medium strong cheese
30 g [1 oz] dried breadcrumbs
5 ml [1 tsp] baking powder
5 ml [1 tsp] ground allspice
45 ml [3 tbsp] chopped parsley
4 size 2 [large] eggs

This traditional North African dish involves such long and tedious preparation that I never bothered to cook it until I acquired a food processor. Thanks to this, it is now very easy to prepare. A pressure cooker also saves an enormous amount of time.

1 Rinse the chickpeas and soak them in plenty of water for at least 8 hours.

2 Chop one of the onions finely and put it in the pressure cooker or a saucepan with a tablespoonful of oil. Set over medium heat, and cook with the lid off. Trim the beef, cut it into even chunks and add it to the pan. Brown it on all sides for about 10 minutes. Meanwhile, drain the chickpeas, reserving the soaking water, and rub off the skins if necessary.

3 Add the chickpeas to the pan and pour in enough of the soaking water to cover them to a depth of 3 cm [1 in.]. Add pepper (but no salt yet) and ground cinnamon. Cover the pan, bring the pressure up and cook for about 20 minutes (or about 2 hours in a saucepan). The meat should be tender enough to cut with a fork; if it isn't, simmer for a while with the lid half covering the pan. There should be a reasonable amount of fairly thick sauce. Adjust the amount of liquid by either continuing to cook the meat uncovered or by adding water to the sauce. Add salt to taste.

4 Preheat the oven to moderate, 180°C [350°F, gas 4]. Process the minced lamb, remaining onion, most of the cheese and the breadcrumbs to a soft, even purée consistency. Transfer to a mixing bowl, add the baking powder, ground allspice and chopped parsley, then beat in the eggs one by one.

* This dish can be prepared in advance to this stage.

5 Put the beef and chickpeas in a medium-sized ovenproof dish: they should cover the bottom in one layer. Spread the processed mixture over the top. Sprinkle the rest of the grated cheese over it and bake in the oven for 30 to 40 minutes, until the mixture is set and the top is brown. Serve hot or cold with bread and a salad.

LAMB STEW FOR COUSCOUS

PREPARATION TIME
8 hours soaking
2 hours 10 minutes, including
 1 hour 50 minutes cooking

20 g [¾ oz] chickpeas
30 ml [2 tbsp] oil
1 medium onion
600 g [1½ lb] stewing lamb
4 medium tomatoes
2 cloves garlic
5 ml [1 tsp] ground ginger
5 ml [1 tsp] crushed fennel
 seeds
4 ml [scant 1 tsp] turmeric
4 ml [scant 1 tsp] harissa or
 other red chilli sauce
1 teacupful water
1 medium carrot
1 large courgette
4 small potatoes
1 recipe precooked couscous
 (see right)

This lamb stew is one of an infinite variety that go with couscous. It is advisable to start by preparing the couscous according to the recipe on page 108, giving it the second steaming over this stew.

1 Cover the chickpeas with water and leave to soak for at least 8 hours.
2 Pour the oil into the bottom part of a couscous steamer or into a large, heavy-based saucepan. Chop the onion very finely. Trim the meat and cut it into 5 cm [2 in.] cubes. Cook the meat and onion gently in the oil for about 30 minutes, turning occasionally.
3 Skin, deseed and chop the tomatoes. Crush the garlic and pound to a paste with the ginger, fennel seeds and turmeric. Mix with the tomatoes and chilli sauce. (A food processor is ideal for this.)
4 Turn up the heat to brown the meat, then add the tomato and spice mixture, chickpeas and a teacupful of water. Bring to the boil, turn down the heat, half cover and simmer for about 1 hour.
5 Scrape and cut the carrot and courgette into large chunks. Leave the potatoes whole, peeled or unpeeled as you prefer. Add the vegetables to the mixture and leave to simmer for about 20 minutes.
6 Put the precooked couscous (prepared to the end of step 3 of the recipe on page 108) in the top of the steamer and fit the two halves snugly together. Steam the couscous uncovered for 20 minutes, fluffing it up occasionally with a fork.
7 Warm a large serving dish. When the vegetables are tender, add salt to taste. Spoon the couscous into the serving dish, making a pile with a hollow in the centre. Trickle some of the sauce over the couscous. Spoon some of the meat and sauce into the hollow in the centre, and scatter a few pieces of the vegetables on to the mound. Serve the rest of the stew in a separate bowl.

For a different flavour, add a bouquet of parsley and fresh coriander to the stew with the tomato and spice mixture. Remove just before serving.

LAHME LAHLOU (SWEET MEAT)

PREPARATION TIME
3–4 hours soaking
1 hour 10 minutes, including 1
 hour cooking

125 g [4 oz] prunes
125 g [4 oz] sugar
30 ml [2 tbsp] orange flower
 water
2.5 ml [½ tsp] ground cinnamon
450 g [1 lb] lean lamb, either
 fillet or cut from the leg or
 shoulder

TO GARNISH
30 g [1 oz] blanched almonds

This is served in Algeria at the end of a meal, on very special occasions. It is eaten on its own, as the crowning moment of the meal; you might compare it to mediaeval mincemeat and blancmange, both of which were festive sweet dishes made with meat.

1 Rinse the prunes and soak in water for at least 3 or 4 hours.
2 Put half the sugar, half the orange flower water and the ground cinnamon into a heavy-based saucepan and heat gently for a few minutes.
3 Meanwhile, cut the meat into 5 cm [2 in.] cubes. Add to the saucepan and cook slowly for about 45 minutes or until tender, checking from time to time and adding a little water if necessary. When the meat is cooked, the sauce should have thickened to a syrupy consistency.
4 Grill the almonds gently until lightly coloured and set aside. Stone the prunes and add them with the rest of the sugar to the pan and simmer for about 10 minutes. Just before serving, stir in the remaining orange flower water. Taste, and adjust the seasoning. Serve garnished with roasted almonds.

OPPOSITE Lamb Stew for Couscous (*left*) and Lahme Lahlou, an Algerian sweet meat

> SAUCES
> Middle Eastern sauces, whether on their own, in stews or similar dishes, are seldom thickened by adding flour. Instead they are reduced to the correct thickness, which also intensifies the flavour.
>   Onions used in sauces should always be chopped extremely finely or even grated so that when the sauce is cooked, the onions should be invisible. Always begin cooking them over a low or medium heat until transparent and soft. Then the heat can be turned up if you want to brown them.

VEGETABLES & PULSES

As a child, the only cooked fresh vegetables I ever ate were *bamia* (okra) in sauce, *melokheya* (see page 42) – and chips! Other vegetables, especially when simply cooked, I always dismissed as food for the sick. Now, after years of cooking, I have developed quite a taste for vegetables, and the more simply cooked the better.

However, simple cooking does not just mean boiling, as you can see from the recipes that follow. I usually cook vegetables in a little oil and flavouring, with hardly any water. A basic rule is that the younger and fresher the vegetable, the simpler the flavouring should be. The simplest of all is olive oil, salt (sea salt is best) and lime or lemon juice. To these might be added a little garlic, turmeric and chopped celery leaves or parsley or fresh coriander leaves; or some spices such as roasted and roughly crushed coriander seed, caraway seed, a very little harissa, ginger (fresh or powdered) or just a little chilli powder.

In the Middle East fresh vegetables are usually cooked in stews made with meat, poultry or fish, and so some vegetable recipes – those with a higher proportion of meat or other ingredients – will be found in other chapters. But vegetables are also cooked and eaten without meat, when they are just as varied and interesting. Fresh vegetables combine marvellously with pulses. There are also many superb recipes for stuffed vegetables to be eaten cold or hot. It is easy to put a number of dishes together for a well-balanced and exciting vegetarian meal.

Clockwise from top left Shredded Cabbage, Braised New Potatoes, French Bean Stew and Okra with Veal, with a bowl of Preserved Lemons (*recipe on page 139*) and pickled cucumbers

BRAISED NEW POTATOES

PREPARATION TIME
15 minutes, including at least
10 minutes cooking

15–30 ml [1–2 tbsp] oil
1 clove garlic
30 ml [2 tbsp] water
500 g [or 1 lb] new potatoes
sea salt to taste
juice of ½–1 lemon

(picture on page 84)

1 Choose a heavy-based saucepan into which the potatoes will fit in one layer. Put in just enough oil to line the base of the pan and set it over a low heat. Finely slice in the garlic and add, with a couple of tablespoonfuls of water.
2 Wash and scrub the potatoes and put them in the pan. Add salt and lemon juice, put the lid on the pan and shake well to coat the potatoes. Cook, covered, over low heat until cooked; this may take as little as 10 minutes, but new potatoes are surprisingly variable. Check every 5 minutes or so to make sure that the liquid does not completely dry up before the potatoes are cooked. If necessary add a little more water, cover the pan again and shake.

OLD POTATOES can be cooked in the same way, but first cut them into chunks and half cover them with water.

SHREDDED CABBAGE

PREPARATION TIME
10–15 minutes, including
cooking

15–30 ml [1–2 tbsp] oil
15 ml [1 tbsp] tomato purée
salt to taste
30 ml [2 tbsp] water
1 medium white or solid green
cabbage, about 1 kg [2 lb]
15 ml [1 tbsp] coriander seed

(picture on page 84)

1 Coat the base of a large heavy-based saucepan with oil. Stir in the tomato purée, salt and a couple of tablespoonfuls of water, and set over a low heat.
2 Shred the cabbage thickly and add it to the saucepan in batches; each batch will soften a little and make room for the next batch when that is ready. Stir thoroughly to mix in the sauce. Cover the pan and simmer gently. Meanwhile, dry roast the coriander seed, crush it roughly and add to the pan, stirring thoroughly. Continue simmering for a few minutes until the cabbage is cooked to your taste.

CABBAGE AND LAMB CASSEROLE Put alternate layers of shredded cabbage mixed with 1 grated medium onion and slices of lamb fillet into an ovenproof casserole, finishing with a layer of cabbage. Preheat the oven to moderate, 180°C [350°F, gas 4]. Mix 2 tablespoonfuls of oil with salt and pepper in a bowl with a little boiling water. Barely cover the cabbage with this mixture. Cook for 1 hour. Just before serving, fry a little paprika in a tablespoonful of oil and pour over the top.

A Moroccan stall stacked with beautifully arranged vegetables. They include *kabak* (large courgettes), aubergines, globe artichokes and white radishes as well as the more familiar carrots, cauliflowers and spinach; a string of fennel bulbs hangs from the stall. The stall owner is sitting on a box of green chillis; by his side are large bunches of flat-leafed parsley.

VEGETABLE STEWS

As you will have gathered from the poultry and meat chapters, Middle Eastern stews are often a combination of meat or poultry cooked with vegetables in varying proportions. Once again, the cooking of vegetable stews is fairly simple, and variety comes from the choice and proportions of ingredients and from the various flavourings and seasonings. All the stews with meat in this chapter are also often cooked without it.

FRENCH BEAN STEW

PREPARATION TIME
25 minutes, including 15 minutes cooking

1 recipe Tomato Sauce or Meat and Tomato Sauce (see page 138)
500 g–1 kg [1–2 lb] French beans (see right)
salt and pepper to taste

(picture on page 85)

I was a teenager before I reluctantly agreed to taste a vegetable stew for the first time. It was a heavily-peppered French bean dish. I had to concede – despite myself – that I liked it. Even now, French beans in tomato sauce are not quite right for me without a lot of pepper.

1 Start with a basic Tomato, or Meat and Tomato, sauce (see page 137). If you are using the Meat and Tomato Sauce, you will need only 500 g [1 lb] of beans. Top and tail the beans and add to the sauce with salt and lots of pepper, tasting to check that you have the right amount. Barely cover the beans with water, bring to the boil, lower the heat and simmer, covered, for 10 minutes or until cooked to your liking.
2 If you like crisp vegetables, the beans will be ready while the sauce is still quite liquid. I like them when they just lose their bright green colour. Remove and reserve the beans while you reduce the sauce to a good thick consistency, then return them to the pan, reheat if necessary and serve.

OKRA WITH VEAL

PREPARATION TIME
30 minutes soaking
1 hour, including 30 minutes cooking

500 g [1 lb] okra
½ teacupful vinegar
30 ml [2 tbsp] oil
1 small onion
250 g [8 oz] veal, cut from the shoulder or knuckle
5 ml [1 tsp] coriander seed
30 ml [2 tbsp] tomato purée
salt and pepper to taste
juice of 1 lemon

(picture on page 85)

1 Wash and top the okra pods. Soak them in vinegar and water for 30 minutes (see below), rinse, drain and leave to dry, or dry with kitchen paper, and set aside.
2 Coat the base of a medium saucepan with oil. Finely chop or grate the onion, add to the pan and cook on medium heat until soft and transparent. Cut the meat into 3 cm [1 in.] chunks, add to the pan, raise the heat and turn the meat to brown it. Meanwhile gently dry roast the coriander seed in a separate pan and crush it. When the meat is browned all over, add tomato purée, salt and pepper to taste, the roasted coriander and lemon juice and enough water to just cover the meat. Bring to the boil, lower the heat to simmer, cover and leave to cook for about 15 minutes, or until the meat is very tender.
3 Cut each okra pod into two or three pieces and add to the pan. If the liquid is drying up, add a little water. Simmer for another 10 to 15 minutes, or until the okra is cooked. If the liquid is too watery, reduce it to a thick sauce. Taste, adjust the seasoning and serve. This dish is best served with rice.

Instead of lemon juice, you might like to add a teaspoonful of crushed dried limes.

Using a very sharp knife, peel off a thin layer of the stem, following its cone shape.

> PREPARING OKRA
> Larger okra tends to have a slimy texture when cooked, which some people find unpleasant. There are a couple of ways of avoiding this. The first is not to cut into the okra, which is why the stem should be peeled in a cone shape without removing it completely (see left). I have also recently discovered the following tip, which I find very effective. Peel the okra, soak it in vinegar (about 1 teacupful per 500 g [1 lb]) and water to cover for about 30 minutes, then rinse and dry.

CAULIFLOWER IN TOMATO SAUCE

PREPARATION TIME
45 minutes, including 15 minutes cooking

1 cauliflower, about 1 kg [2 lb]
very fine dry breadcrumbs
oil for generous shallow frying
1 recipe Tomato Sauce (see page 137)
a sparing teacupful water

Cauliflower, like French beans (see page 87), is delicious cooked in tomato sauce; but it needs a slightly different preparation.

1 Cut the cauliflower into small florets, blanch them in boiling water, or steam them for a minute or so, and refresh under cold water. Then roll them in very fine breadcrumbs, fry in the oil until golden, and drain on kitchen paper.
2 Pour away most of the oil in the pan, leaving about a tablespoonful of oil and any remaining breadcrumbs. Pour in the Tomato Sauce, stirring well, and add a small cupful of water, then the cauliflower, gently turning it over to coat the pieces with sauce. Taste and adjust the seasoning if necessary, bring to the boil and simmer until the sauce has thickened.

SPICED CARROTS

PREPARATION TIME
30 minutes, including 15–20 minutes cooking

15 ml [1 tbsp] oil
1 kg [2 lb] carrots
2–3 cloves garlic
5 ml [1 tsp] crushed caraway seed
30 ml [2 tbsp] vinegar
salt to taste
a small dot harissa or other red chilli sauce (optional)

1 Line the base of a medium saucepan with a thin layer of oil. Scrub and slice the carrots and put them in the pan to cook over a medium heat.
2 Finely chop the garlic and add to the pan with crushed caraway seed and the vinegar. Stir. Add salt, a small dot of harissa if you like, and enough water to barely cover the carrots. Cover and reduce the heat to simmer. Leave to cook until the carrots are tender, shaking the pan occasionally to prevent sticking. Check that the liquid does not completely dry up before the carrots are cooked. If necessary, add a little more water. Serve hot.

You can also mash the carrots to a purée and serve cold. This makes an excellent *mezze* (see page 27).

COURGETTES IN SAUCE

PREPARATION TIME
30–45 minutes, including 15–30 minutes cooking

6 medium courgettes, about 750 g [or 1½ lb] in all
½ tomato
15 ml [1 tbsp] tomato purée
about 1 teacupful water
15 ml [1 tbsp] oil
salt and pepper to taste

TA'LEYA
2 cloves garlic
oil for shallow frying
10 ml [2 tsp] crushed coriander seed

Our cook in Cairo always served vegetables such as courgettes, okra or French beans arranged in a pretty pattern. She laid them in this pattern in the pan before cooking, then turned them out in one piece on to the serving dish. But in fact this recipe is delightful no matter how it is presented.

1 Top and tail, wash and dry the courgettes. Cut them diagonally into 1 cm [⅜ in.] slices. Choose a saucepan which will hold 2 or 3 layers and arrange the slices in it, tightly overlapping in neat circles, leaving a small hole in the middle. Into this hole put half a tomato, skin side down.
2 Mix the tomato purée with the water and oil, add salt and pepper and carefully pour over the courgettes. The liquid should barely cover them. Take a plate that will fit fairly closely inside the pan, wrap it in foil and invert it over the courgettes (the foil will act as a handle so that you can lift out the plate). Press the plate down and put the lid on the pan. Bring the mixture to a gentle boil, turn the heat down to simmer and cook for 15 to 30 minutes or until the courgettes are tender.
3 Meanwhile prepare a Ta'leya in a frying pan. Chop the garlic very finely and fry quickly in a little oil with the crushed coriander seed until lightly coloured.
4 Remove the lid and the plate from the courgettes. Spoon a little of the liquid from the courgettes on to the Ta'leya, mix and return to the pan. If the sauce is too liquid, raise the heat and reduce to thicken it as much as possible. Cover the pan with a large round serving dish. Then, with gloved hands, very carefully but swiftly invert the pan so that its contents fall out on to the dish. With luck (and practice) there should be a pretty circle of courgette slices with a domed red tomato centre.

OPPOSITE Spiced Carrots (*top*), Cauliflower in Tomato Sauce (*centre left*), Courgettes in Sauce (*bottom*) and Rich Pilaf Rice (*recipe on page 104*)

You can add a dash of harissa or other chilli sauce, and a squeeze of lemon juice to the Ta'leya. Any leftovers can be mashed with a fork and served as a *mezze* the following day. They are equally delicious served cold like this.

MIXED VEGETABLE TAJINE

This belongs to the same tradition as the French 'ratatouille'.

PREPARATION TIME
40–55 minutes, including
  25–30 minutes cooking

1 medium onion
1 lemon
30 ml [2 tbsp] oil
2–3 carrots
120 g [4 oz] each French
  beans, peas and broad beans,
  fresh or frozen (weight
  without pods)
salt and pepper to taste
5 ml [1 tsp] ground allspice
45 ml [3 tbsp] chopped fresh
  coriander

1 Chop the onion finely and slice the lemon. Pour the oil into a large, heavy-based saucepan, add the onion and lemon and set over a low heat. Add the rest of the vegetables as you go along. Scrub and slice the carrots, top and tail the French beans, and pod the broad beans and peas if using fresh ones. Frozen vegetables should be added straight from the freezer. Add salt, pepper, ground allspice and most of the chopped coriander leaves, keeping some back to garnish the finished dish.
2 Add enough water to barely cover the vegetables; if they are frozen, however, there will be enough water without adding any. Bring to the boil, then lower the heat to simmer. Cook, uncovered, until the vegetables are just tender, about 20 minutes. Sprinkle with the rest of the chopped coriander and serve with rice.

Other combinations of vegetables are also very good cooked in this way. Peas, broad beans and artichoke hearts, for example, make a superb mixture. If you like, meat balls can be added before the second stage of cooking or the flavour varied with a little chilli powder or sauce, or a Ta'leya (see page 140). You can also omit the lemon.

CELERY, COURGETTES AND CHICKPEAS

Mixtures of pulses and fresh vegetables are extremely popular in the Middle East. The balance of flavours, shapes, colours and textures also makes good nutritional sense to vegetarians.

PREPARATION TIME
8 hours soaking
1 hour 20 minutes–2 hours 20
  minutes, including cooking

120 g [4 oz] chickpeas
1 large onion
15 ml [1 tbsp] oil
30 ml [2 tbsp] tomato purée
4–5 sticks celery
salt and pepper to taste
2 medium courgettes

(picture on page 96)

1 Wash the chickpeas well, cover with water and leave to soak for 8 hours.
2 Grate the onion and cook slowly in oil until transparent and soft. Add the tomato purée and cook a little longer, then add the chickpeas and their soaking water. Bring to the boil, lower the heat and simmer until done, 1 to 2 hours depending on the chickpeas. (If you use a pressure cooker they will take about 20 minutes.)
3 Trim and wash the celery and cut it into 3 cm [1 in.] pieces. When the chickpeas are tender, add the celery, season with salt and pepper and simmer for another 15 minutes, or until the celery is just done: it should still be quite firm. Wash the courgettes, slice them thickly and add to the pan. Cook for another 5 minutes.
4 If there is too much liquid left, remove the vegetables to a serving bowl with a slotted spoon, reduce the liquid to a thickish sauce and pour it over them.

This dish can be varied by using different vegetables, such as spinach instead of courgettes: chop the spinach or tear it up roughly and add at the same stage.
    For a spicy flavour, add a little ground ginger and crushed garlic, and a pinch of chilli powder.
    Another very popular mixture cooked in the same way is lentils and spinach, which go particularly well together (omit the celery). Just before serving, stir in a little yoghurt.
    Non-vegetarians can also start by cooking pieces of meat with the onion, or by adding small meat balls before the celery.

SOAKING PULSES
The length of soaking time for pulses varies a great deal, and depends on how long the pulses have been stored since they were dried. Check that they are adequately soaked by biting a bean (or chickpea, etc.). It is ready to cook when it is soft enough to chew.
    If you are really pushed for time, you could use canned pulses instead of the dried variety, but I would not personally recommend it.

OPPOSITE Mixed Vegetable Tajine (*top*), Stuffed Vine Leaves (*right*) and Foul Medames (*recipe on page 100*)

STUFFING VINE LEAVES

  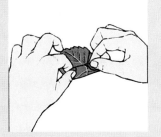 

1 Place a neat, sausage-shaped pile of stuffing on the leaf, just above the division at its base.

2 Fold each side of the leaf diagonally into the centre so that they overlap over the stuffing.

3 Start rolling the leaf from the base to the tip, then fold the two sides into the centre. Continue rolling and folding in this way until you have an even, sausage-shaped package.

4 Tightly pack the vine leaves, with the fold sides underneath, into the saucepan with the larger packages in the centre and the smaller ones in circles around them.

STUFFED VINE LEAVES

PREPARATION TIME

30 minutes soaking

1½ hours, including 30 minutes cooking

STUFFING

120 g [4 oz] uncooked short grain rice

60 g [2 oz] raisins

3–4 medium dried apricots

2–3 spring onions

60 ml [4 tbsp] finely chopped parsley

45 ml [3 tbsp] finely chopped fresh coriander leaves

60 g [2 oz] broken walnuts, roughly chopped

salt and pepper to taste

30 ml [2 tbsp] crushed dried dill weed

15 ml [1 tbsp] crushed dried mint

5 ml [1 tsp] ground cinnamon

5 ml [1 tsp] ground allspice

30–45 ml [2–3 tbsp] oil

250 g [8 oz] fresh or preserved vine leaves (about 2 dozen)

30–45 ml [2–3 tbsp] oil

15 ml [1 tbsp] tomato purée

salt and pepper to taste

juice of 2 lemons or limes

2 cloves garlic

(picture on page 91)

I always used to cook vine leaves with a meat stuffing until I tried this Persian-inspired herb, nut and fruit mixture. The dish should always be eaten cold so that the delicate flavours of the stuffing have a chance to blend.

1 Make the stuffing. Wash and drain the rice. Pour boiling water over the raisins and apricots and leave to soak for 10 minutes.

2 Drain the apricots and raisins, reserving the soaking water, and chop the apricots finely. Chop the spring onions, including the green tops, very finely. Put all these in a bowl with the rice and the chopped parsley, coriander and walnuts. Mix together, then add salt, pepper, the crushed herbs, ground cinnamon and allspice and 2 or 3 tablespoons of oil. There should be just enough oil to make the mixture glisten when you have given it another thorough mixing.

3 If you are using fresh vine leaves, blanch them in boiling water for less than 1 minute, just long enough to soften them. If using preserved vine leaves, rinse them well and blanch for 3 or 4 minutes. In either case blanching time depends on the age of the leaves: they should be tender enough to bite through but they should not tear. Rinse the leaves well in cold water, and drain on kitchen paper, and sort them out by size.

4 Choose a broad saucepan with a tight-fitting lid, which will hold all the stuffed leaves in a single tight layer, or at most two layers. Line it with three or four of the thickest and largest leaves, and any unsuitably small or broken ones. Stuff all the other leaves with filling, folding and rolling them into small, neat packages as shown in the illustration above. Make sure that the filling will stay in a compact pile before you start rolling. Pack the pan tightly, with the larger leaves in the centre and smaller ones arranged in circles around them. Beat 2 to 3 tablespoonfuls of oil in a cup with tomato purée, salt, pepper and lemon juice. Pour this all over the leaves, and add some of the soaking water from the fruit until they are barely covered. Finely slice the garlic and insert slices between the stuffed leaves.

5 Bring to the boil. Cover the top of the largest plate that will fit inside the pan with a sheet of foil. Put it in the pan upside down, so that the corners of the foil form a handle for lifting the plate out.

6 Put the lid on, lower the heat and leave the stuffed vine leaves to simmer for about 1 hour, or until the largest packages in the centre are cooked. The only way to tell if they are done is to taste one. Adjust the flavouring of the sauce: it may well need more lemon juice.

7 Serve cold. If you try one hot and another one later, you will notice how the flavours have blended into full harmony.

Vine leaves can also be stuffed with a meat filling, such as the one used for stuffing leeks (opposite), for instance. They are often served as part of a *mezze* spread, with tahina and other dips.

STUFFED LEEKS

PREPARATION TIME
10 minutes soaking
1 hour, including 30–45
    minutes cooking

8–10 medium-sized dried
    apricots

STUFFING
60 g [2 oz] uncooked short
    grain rice
1 medium onion
250 g [or 8 oz] minced lamb
45 ml [3 tbsp] chopped parsley
15 ml [1 tbsp] crushed dried
    mint
salt and pepper to taste

2 large leeks
30–45 ml [2–3 tbsp] oil
salt and pepper to taste
juice of 1 lemon

(picture on page 95)

1 Pour boiling water over the apricots and leave them to soak for about 10 minutes.
2 Make the stuffing. Wash the rice thoroughly and drain it. Grate the onion. Mix the minced lamb with the rice, onion, chopped parsley, crushed mint, salt and pepper together. Knead the mixture thoroughly until smooth and set aside.
3 Discard any discoloured outer leaves from the leeks and cut off the untidy tops and the solid bases. With a very sharp knife, cut each leek open lengthways to the centre. Follow the step-by-step instructions below. Open out the leaves and wash thoroughly in cold water.
4 Drain the apricots, reserving the soaking liquid. Chop the apricots very finely. Chop the small, innermost leaves of the leeks very finely and mix with the apricots. Add a couple of tablespoonfuls of this mixture to the stuffing and reserve the rest.
5 Choose a large, heavy-based saucepan that will hold all the stuffed leeks in a single layer, or two layers at the most. Chop the coarse outer leaves of the leeks and line the pan with them. Cut the rest of the leaves into 5 cm [2 in.] lengths. Fill each leaf with a small, sausage-shaped roll of filling slightly shorter than the cut section of leaf, and wrap it up to make a roll (rather like cannelloni). With those pieces of leaf too small to go around the filling, close one piece partly around the filling, then put another piece on the other side to completely cover it. The curl of the leaf will keep the package together. Gently fry the rolls of leek in a little oil in a frying pan, taking care that they do not unravel – which is easier than you might think. When they are golden, transfer them to the saucepan, packing them closely and neatly with the larger rolls in the centre.
6 Pour away any oil left in the frying pan, add the leek and apricot mixture, cook quickly on a fairly high heat, stirring constantly, for a minute or so; then add the soaking water, salt, pepper and lemon juice. Pour this mixture over the leeks in the saucepan; they should be just covered. Set the pan on the stove, bring to the boil and lower the heat to simmer. Cover the leeks with an upturned plate wrapped in foil, put on a tight-fitting lid and leave to cook for 30 to 45 minutes. Check from time to time that the liquid is not drying up too quickly: it should have reduced to a good thick sauce by the time the leeks and filling are cooked. If it isn't thick enough, reduce quickly with the lid off the pan. Serve warm or cold.

STUFFED COURGETTES The recipe for leeks is actually an adaptation of a traditional one for courgettes, whose flavour also goes very well with the sweet and sour apricot filling. Make the stuffing as above. Cut each courgette in half crossways and hollow it out with an apple corer, reserving the scooped-out middle. Chop this and add to the apricots for the sauce, as above. Push the filling in to the hollow courgettes, not too tightly and leaving a little gap at each end to allow for the rice to expand as it cooks.

STUFFING LEEKS

1 Cut off the top leaves and bases, then cut to the centre of the leek all along its length.

2 Open out the leaves and wash thoroughly. Cut them into 5cm (2 in.) lengths.

3 Stuff the larger leaves first. Put a roll of filling along the leaf which will naturally curl itself over to cover it.

4 To stuff the smaller leaves, put the filling along one leaf, then place another leaf on top to enclose the filling.

STUFFED LETTUCE LEAVES

PREPARATION TIME
2 hours, including 1 hour
    cooking

12 outer leaves of cos or
    Webb's lettuce
3 large slices white bread made
    into soft crumbs
500 g [1 lb] minced beef
2 eggs
salt and pepper to taste
flour for coating
oil for shallow frying
1 teacupful meat broth
juice of $\frac{1}{2}$–1 lemon, to taste

I had never thought cooked lettuce leaves could be nice until I was given this Sephardic recipe from Salonika by Mrs Bondi Attas.

1 Carefully remove a dozen large, sound leaves from the lettuce and blanch them for 5 minutes in lightly salted boiling water. Refresh under cold water and drain on kitchen paper.
2 Make the stuffing. Mix the breadcrumbs with the minced beef and one of the eggs, season with salt and pepper and knead well.
3 Take an egg-sized ball of the stuffing and place it on the stem end of the leaf. Begin rolling it up towards the tip. Fold the sides in to make a parcel, then roll up completely. Beat the remaining egg. Roll each stuffed leaf in flour, then dip it in egg.
4 Choose a broad pan with a tight-fitting lid, which is large enough to hold all the stuffed leaves in one compact layer. Pour in enough oil to coat the bottom generously, and set it over fairly high heat. When hot, put in the stuffed leaves and fry quickly, turning until brown all over. Lower the heat and add meat broth to just cover the stuffed leaves. Add a little lemon juice, cover and simmer for 1 hour.
5 Transfer the stuffed leaves to a serving dish, and keep them warm if necessary while you reduce the liquid in the pan to make a fairly thick sauce, adding more salt, pepper or lemon juice to taste. Pour the sauce over the leaves and serve hot or cold.

SARMA

PREPARATION TIME
3 hours, including $2\frac{1}{4}$ hours
    cooking

STUFFING
2 medium onions
50 g [1$\frac{3}{4}$ oz] bacon
500 g [or 1 lb] mixed minced
    beef and pork
15 ml [1 tbsp] uncooked short
    grain rice
salt and pepper to taste
1 egg

1 medium green cabbage,
    about 1 kg [or 2 lb]
500 g [or 1 lb] smoked pork or
    ham
15 ml [1 tbsp] oil

The recipe for this Yugoslav stuffed cabbage dish was sent to me by Mrs Zagorka Cvejić. Any kind of green cabbage or spring greens is suitable, as long as the leaves can be separated without tearing. For an authentic flavour use smoked pork or ham with quite a strong smoked taste.

1 Finely chop the onions and bacon. Set a little of the onion aside. Use some of the bacon fat to grease a pan, and gently fry the rest of the onion and the bacon until the onion is soft. Add the minced meat, mix and fry until all is well combined. Add the rice, salt, pepper, the rest of the raw onion and the lightly beaten egg. Stir well for a minute or so. Remove from the heat and reserve.
2 Carefully dismantle the cabbage and select about 2 dozen sound, not too coarse leaves. Cut the larger leaves in halves down the middle, removing and reserving the midrib. With medium-sized leaves, pare away the thick part of the midrib, taking care not to cut through the leaf. Blanch the leaves in boiling water until slightly softened. Stuff each leaf by putting some filling in the middle, folding over the stem end, then the tip, and rolling the leaf up sideways to make a cylindrical parcel.
3 Cover the bottom of a heavy-based pan with the rest of the cabbage, including the bits of leaf rib, coarsely chopped. Put half the rolls in the pan, cover with half the smoked pork or ham, cut into thin strips, then add the rest of the rolls and a final layer of pork. Add a tablespoonful of oil and water to just cover, set the pan on the stove and simmer very slowly for about 2 hours. Check occasionally that the liquid is not drying up too quickly, and add a little water if needed. It should have thickened slightly by the end of cooking. Serve hot or cold.
* This dish can be prepared in advance. It reheats very well.

> OTHER STUFFED VEGETABLES
> All kinds of other, sometimes less expected, vegetables can also be stuffed: aubergines, peppers, tomatoes, potatoes or artichokes. They may be cooked on top of the stove or baked – in the Middle East they are sometimes cooked together in a large baking dish so that the flavours of the vegetables and stuffings blend. They are then served hot or cold, often with natural yoghurt or an egg and lemon sauce.

Stuffed Leeks (*left*), Sarma (*top right*) and Stuffed Lettuce Leaves. Stuffed vegetables are often served with natural yoghurt, or a sauce

STUFFED ONIONS

PREPARATION TIME
1 hour 20 minutes, including 1 hour cooking

4 large, mild Spanish onions
1 recipe stuffing (see right)
15 ml [1 tbsp] oil
juice of 1 lemon
salt and pepper to taste
15 ml [1 tbsp] sugar

(*picture on page 99*)

These caramelized stuffed onions are absolutely delicious. Large, mild Spanish onions are the best ones to use.

1 Open the onions out in the same way as leeks: by removing the top and bottom and slicing from one side to the centre. But then blanch them until they soften enough to pull apart. Then fill each 'leaf', which will roll itself naturally around the stuffing. Again, use any stuffing you like: the one on page 93 is my favourite.

2 Pack the rolls in a pan and add a tablespoon of oil, the juice of a lemon, salt, pepper and a tablespoon of sugar. Cook slowly, covered, for at least 1 hour, allowing the liquid to reduce slowly until it caramelizes the onions. They will need to be turned over several times.

3 Transfer the onions carefully to a serving dish (they should be very soft) and spoon over the juices.

LEEK AND POTATO EGGAH

I made up this recipe recently, thinking that leeks and potatoes go very well together; but so do leeks and eggs – a very traditional combination. Like most 'eggahs', this can be baked in a moderate oven for about 45 minutes (see pages 66–7), or cooked in a frying pan as below.

PREPARATION TIME
50 minutes, including 30 minutes cooking

250 g [8 oz] leeks
120 g [4 oz] potatoes
30 ml [2 tbsp] milk
6 size 2 [large] eggs
salt and pepper to taste
120 g [4 oz] Emmenthal or similar cheese
about 30 ml [2 tbsp] clarified butter

1 Wash the leeks thoroughly, discarding any discoloured parts, and dry them. Peel the potatoes, dry them and grate into a mixing bowl. Slice the leeks finely and add them. (A food processor can be used for all the grating and cutting.) Pour in the milk, then stir in (but do not beat) the eggs one by one. Add salt and pepper, and grate in the cheese. Taste, and adjust the seasoning.

2 Heat a frying pan and add enough clarified butter to line it well, swirling it around to coat the sides. When the butter is hot, add the egg mixture. Cover the pan and cook on a very low heat. After 10 or 15 minutes, check that it is not sticking, and slide a metal spatula around the edge. Replace the lid.

3 After about 20 to 25 minutes in all, depending on thickness, the *eggah* should be set, except for the surface. Remove the lid from the pan and put the *eggah* under a medium grill for 2 to 3 minutes, or until the top is set. There is no need to brown it. Serve warm or cold.

To bake the *eggah*, use a moderate oven, 180°C [350°F, gas 4] and allow up to 45 minutes, depending on the depth of mixture in the baking dish.

ABOVE Celery, Courgettes and Chickpeas; Lentils and Rice; Spinach Eggah and Leek and Potato Eggah

SPINACH EGGAH

PREPARATION TIME
1 hour 5 minutes, including 35
    minutes cooking

1 500 g [1 lb] packet frozen
    chopped spinach
salt
60 g [2 oz] butter + more to
    grease dish or frying pan
25 ml [1 heaped tbsp] flour
about 120 ml [4 fl oz] milk
60–80 g [2–3 oz] grated
    cheese, to taste
breadcrumbs for coating dish
4–5 size 2 [large] eggs
salt, pepper, grated nutmeg and
    ground allspice to taste

1 Put the spinach and salt in a heavy-based pan over a low heat to thaw slowly. Add the butter. When it has melted, raise the heat to make sure that all the water has evaporated from the spinach. Squash with a spoon and sprinkle in the flour and stir thoroughly. The flour will absorb any extra moisture; make sure there are no lumps.

2 Stir in the milk a little at a time, making sure that it is thoroughly blended in before you add more. As you stir, scrape the bottom and sides of the pan to make sure the mixture is not sticking.

3 Add the grated cheese. The quantity of cheese depends on its strength and your preference. Carry on cooking gently until the mixture has a dry purée consistency, dropping but not runny. Leave to cool.

* The dish can be prepared in advance to this stage.

4 If you are baking the *eggah*, preheat the oven to moderate, 180°C [350°F, gas 4]. Heat a baking sheet in the oven. Choose a fairly shallow dish, such as a quiche dish, which the mixture will about half fill; it must not come more than two-thirds of the way up. Butter the dish and coat it thoroughly with breadcrumbs, shaking off the excess.

5 Stir the eggs, one at a time, into the spinach mixture. Check the seasoning, and add salt, pepper, a little nutmeg or allspice as you like. Pour into the dish.

6 Put the dish on the hot baking sheet in the oven and bake for 35 minutes. It is done when the centre is firm to the touch. It may need another 5 or 10 minutes. Alternatively, pour the *eggah* mixture into a buttered, preheated frying pan and cook over a low heat for 10 minutes or longer until it is risen and set firm all through. Brown the top under the grill before serving, or turn it in the frying pan and leave to cook for 1 minute on the other side.

PULSES

HARICOT BEANS WITH EGGS IN RICH MEAT STOCK

PREPARATION TIME
8 hours soaking and overnight cooling
1 hour 10 minutes, including 60 minutes cooking

500 g [1 lb] haricot beans
1 cow's foot or 2 calf's feet
2 large onions
30 ml [2 tbsp] oil
4 eggs
salt to taste

This was one of my favourite childhood dishes. The quantities are rather large for four people, but this dish reheats beautifully and can also be frozen. It can be a bit time-consuming to make, but a large pressure cooker speeds things up. If you do not have one, you will need to multiply the cooking times by 4. Cow's feet are not always available, but it is worth while asking your butcher to order one. They are usually cut and split so that they fit into a saucepan.

1 Wash the beans thoroughly, cover with plenty of water and leave to soak for at least 8 hours.

2 Wash the cow's foot and wipe it with kitchen paper or a tea towel. Any bone splinters will stick to the towel. Put the foot in the pressure cooker and cover it with cold water. Bring to the boil, uncovered, and skim off the scum several times. When you have got rid of all the scum, put the lid on, bring up the pressure and cook for 15 minutes. Strain and reserve the cooking liquid. When the pieces of foot are cool enough to handle, remove all the bones and return the meat (if any) to the liquid. Refrigerate and remove the fat set on the surface.

3 Chop the onions very finely and cook them gently in a little oil in the bottom of the pressure cooker until well softened. Raise the heat and brown them, stirring, until dark brown. Add the meat, its liquid and the drained beans. The liquid should cover the beans by about 5 cm [2 in.] – but make sure you don't fill the pressure cooker above its recommended limit, which is usually half full. Add the eggs in their shells, nested into the beans. Fix on the lid, bring the pressure up and cook for 15 minutes. The beans should now be cooked, but whether they are or not, the flavour will improve with extra simmering, half covered, for at least another 30 minutes.

4 When ready to serve, there should not be more than 1 cm [$\frac{3}{8}$ in.] of broth above the beans, which should be tender. Add salt. Serve with Plain Pilaf Rice (see page 104). The eggs are peeled and seasoned at the table. Although the combination of rice and beans is unexpectedly delicious, I like to add the contrasting texture of a green salad.

HARICOT BEANS FOR VEGETARIANS Soak the beans as in step 1. Then cook from step 3, ignoring references to the meat, but doubling the amount of onions.

YUGOSLAV BAKED BEANS

PREPARATION TIME
8 hours soaking
2$\frac{1}{2}$ hours, including 2 hours cooking

500 g [1 lb] haricot beans
3 large onions
60 ml [4 tbsp] oil
2 fresh chillis
15 ml [1 tbsp] paprika
salt to taste

1 Rinse the beans until the water runs clear, then cover with water and leave to soak for 8 hours.

2 Put the beans with their soaking liquid in a saucepan, and bring to the boil. Finely chop one onion. When the water boils, lower the heat, spoon off the scum, add the onion and half cover the pan. Simmer till the beans are cooked; if they are fresh they will take about 1 hour, but if they are older it can take up to 3 hours. From time to time, add more water as necessary to keep the beans just covered. (A pressure cooker will take about a quarter of the cooking time.)

3 Slice the other two onions into rings and gently fry them in oil till soft and transparent. Add the whole chillis, the paprika and enough salt for the beans as well.

4 Preheat the oven to 190°C [375°F, gas 5]. When the beans are done, put a layer of onions in a baking dish, then a layer of beans, then more onions, finishing with a layer of beans. Pour on the cooking liquid, and bake for about 1 hour, or until the beans are brown and gooey from the melting browned onions. Remove the chillis.

5 Serve hot or cold. Though very good as a hot vegetable dish with a main course, beans cooked in this way are more usually eaten cold as a first course. A small bowl of them makes an ideal addition to a *mezze* spread.

* This dish can be prepared in advance and will keep for up to a week in the refrigerator.

OPPOSITE (*left to right*) Yugoslav Baked Beans, Stuffed Onions and Haricot Beans with Eggs in Rich Meat Stock

LENTILS AND RICE

PREPARATION TIME
30 minutes soaking
**35 minutes–1 hour 5 minutes,
   including cooking**

120 g [4 oz] brown lentils
230 g [8 oz] long grain rice
salt and pepper to taste
15–30 ml [1–2 tbsp] oil
1 large onion
**30 ml [2 tbsp] clarified butter or
   oil**

TO SERVE (optional)
**15 ml [1 tbsp] dry roasted
   sesame seeds**
**1 140 g [5 oz] carton natural
   yoghurt**
5 ml [1 tsp] crushed dried mint
a pinch chilli powder

(picture on page 96)

1 Pick over the lentils and remove any small stones or debris. Wash them thoroughly until the water runs clear. Wash the rice well and leave to soak for at least 30 minutes. If you suspect that the lentils are old and tough, soak them too.

2 Choose a heavy-based saucepan which the lentils and rice will no more than half fill. Put in the lentils, cover them with water to a depth of at least 3 cm [1 in.], bring to the boil, lower the heat, cover and simmer until they are tender. This could take anything between 15 minutes and 1 hour, depending on the age of the lentils, so check from time to time. Add more water if necessary.

3 When the lentils are done, strain the rice and add to the lentils. Add salt, pepper, a tablespoonful or two of oil, and top up the pan with water to cover the mixture up to the top joint of your thumb. Bring to the boil, lower the heat to simmer, cover and cook for about 15 minutes without lifting the lid. See if the rice is done; if not, replace the lid and cook for a few more minutes.

4 Thinly slice the onion into rings and fry them in very hot clarified butter or oil until brown and crisp. Drain on kitchen paper. Serve the rice and lentils in a large dish with the onion rings on top. If you like, sprinkle with dry roasted sesame seeds and accompany with a side bowl of natural yoghurt, on its own or seasoned with crushed dried mint and a pinch of chilli powder.

FOUL MEDAMES

PREPARATION TIME
8 hours soaking
1½ hours, including cooking

250 g [or 8 oz] foul
4 eggs
brown outside skin of 1 onion

(picture on page 91)

This is the national dish of Egypt, eaten by kings (when such creatures existed) and peasants alike. The pronunciation is 'fool medamess', with the accent on the last syllable. It is consumed at all times of the day: breakfast, lunch and dinner, and between meals, enclosed in Arabic bread as a snack, either cooked at home or bought from street stalls. Many families always have cooked foul in the kitchen and will offer some, whatever the menu. It is a very simply cooked, substantial and nourishing dish. Like all pulses the flavour of these small brown beans improves the longer they are cooked, so a pressure cooker or slow cooker are particularly suitable. Whichever you use, it should be a fairly large one which the beans and water do not more than half fill.

1 Pick over the beans and remove any stones and debris. Wash and rinse well. Soak in plenty of water for at least 8 hours.

2 Put the beans in a saucepan or pressure cooker and cover with about 5 cm [2 in.] of water. Add the whole eggs in their shells, nested into the beans, and the washed brown outer skin of an onion, which will help to give the eggs an attractive colour. Cover and simmer for 1½ hours. (If using a pressure cooker, fix on the lid, bring up the pressure and cook for 15 minutes.)

3 Remove the lid and allow the beans to simmer uncovered until the water is only 2 cm [¾ in.] above the beans. The liquid that is left will resemble a rather thin soup. Remove the onion skins and serve in any of the following ways.

At a meal, the foul is served in a tureen and ladled into soup bowls. All seasoning is done at the table, according to individual taste. Salt, pepper, ground cumin, cayenne pepper, oil and lemon juice, and sometimes butter (which some people prefer to oil and lemon) will always be on the table, together with a bowl of Tahina Dip (see page 16) and an Egyptian Salad (page 25); sometimes some Falafel too (see page 18). Each person seasons the foul to their taste, peels the egg (which has acquired an interesting colour and texture) and, if they like, mashes it into the beans.

For breakfast or as a snack it is seasoned and eaten as a sandwich in Arabic bread.

Leftover foul can be transformed by adding two or three skinned, chopped tomatoes to a Ta'leya (see page 140) while simmering the foul. Fry the mixture briefly and add to the foul. Add salt to taste and simmer for at least 15 minutes to let the flavours blend.

OPPOSITE Pulses commonly used in the Middle East:
1 Red lentils 2 Chickpeas
3 Kidney beans 4 Flaked dried broad beans 5 Unpeeled dried broad beans 6 Foul 7 Brown lentils 8 Peeled dried broad beans 9 Green lentils

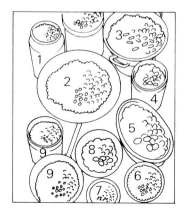

RICE, GRAINS & PASTA

Rice, grains and pasta all form an important part of Middle Eastern fare, though rice is the most universally used. Wheat is also important, not only for bread making; it is often cooked and eaten in the same way as rice. Couscous, a special type of semolina, is specially associated with North Africa, but it is also enjoyed in other Arab countries. Pasta is also much appreciated in most of its forms, and today the Italian influence is to be seen in many Middle Eastern dishes.

Rice is part of the staple diet in many countries of the Middle East. It is cooked on its own or with meats or vegetables, it is also combined with pulses and pasta and it goes into stuffings for fish, poultry and vegetables.

For most of my rice cooking I use Basmati, Patna or any long grain rice. The grains remain whole and separate if properly cooked. However, I prefer short grain rice, Italian or pudding type, for use in stuffings, for exactly the opposite reason: that it clings together. Its softness makes it absorb the flavours of the other ingredients very well.

Although I do recommend soaking rice for a couple of hours before cooking, this is not absolutely essential; but washing the rice should never be omitted.

Clockwise from top left Rice and Broad Beans, Persian Rice with a Crust, Fillet of Lamb Cooked with Rice and Milk and Burghul Pilaf with Aubergine and Cheese

PLAIN PILAF RICE

PREPARATION TIME
2 hours soaking (optional)
30 minutes, including 20
    minutes cooking

1 large teacupful long grain
    (about 230 g [8 oz], but
    measure by volume)
30 g [1 oz] butter or 30 ml [2
    tbsp] oil
1 large teacupful water
salt to taste

There are several recipes for the 'perfect' pilaf. Although some are far from perfect, others do work for some cooks. For instance, I have eaten very good rice made with double the amount of water I use, and cooked in an uncovered pan for part of the time; but whenever I have tried this method, it has failed. So I stick to the methods which are foolproof for me, one of which is given here and the other on page 106. It is important to note that in the pilaf method below the proportion of water to rice increases with the quantity of rice being cooked. Thus, for example, 3 cups of rice require 4 cups of water. For this reason I tend to use the Persian method (page 106) when I am cooking larger amounts of rice since the water does not have to be measured at all.

1   Measure the rice in a large teacup or mug. Wash it well until the water runs clear, then leave to soak for a couple of hours. The soaking is not essential, but the washing is.
2   Drain the rice. Heat the butter or oil in a saucepan, then add a teacupful of water (measured with the cup you used for the rice) and bring it to the boil. As soon as it boils, tip in the rice, add some salt, give it a good stir, and lower the heat to very low: a heat diffuser is advisable. Cover the pan and leave to cook, without lifting the lid, for 20 minutes.
3   Check the rice. It should have absorbed all the water; if so, there will be little holes all over its surface. Take a few grains from the top centre and chew them; they should be tender. If not, replace the lid and cook for a few minutes more. When the rice is ready, let it rest off the heat, covered, for a couple of minutes, then transfer it to a serving dish with a large metal spoon.

The rice can be cooked in stock instead of water, in which case you should omit the butter or oil.

Another method is to gently fry the rice before adding the water. This second method is the one to use for more elaborate pilafs: just before you fry the rice, fry a finely chopped onion with a handful of vermicelli, tomato purée (for pink rice) or turmeric (for yellow rice). You can also make a plain brown and white rice by first frying a small quantity until it starts to brown, then adding the rest of the rice with the water, and proceeding as in the main method.

RICE FOR FISH Measure, wash and soak the rice as above. Heat the oil in a heavy-bottomed saucepan while you finely chop a small onion, and fry it until dark brown. Add a teacupful of water, bring to the boil, then add the drained rice and salt, lower the heat, cover and cook until the rice is done. It should be a nice brown with little black specks; the flavour goes particularly well with fish (*picture on page 51*).

RICH PILAF RICE

PREPARATION TIME
2 hours soaking (optional)
40 minutes, including 30
    minutes cooking

2 teacupfuls long grain rice
    (about 350 g [12 oz], but
    measure by volume)
1 medium onion
15 ml [1 tbsp] oil
225 g [8 oz] chicken liver and
    heart (total weight)
120 g [4 oz] pine nuts
80 g [3 oz] raisins
about 12 cracked cardamom
    pods
10 ml [2 tsp] ground cinnamon
$2\frac{1}{2}$ teacupfuls water

(picture on page 89)

Because of all the additions, it is not worth making a small quantity of this pilaf. The quantities given here would feed 6 people, or 4 with very healthy appetites.
   For a delicious vegetarian dish, simply omit the chicken liver and heart.

1   Measure the rice, using a teacup. Wash it until the water runs clear, then leave to soak in plenty of water for a couple of hours or longer. (Again, the soaking is not essential.)
2   Chop the onion and fry it in the oil in a heavy-based saucepan over a medium heat till soft and brown. Chop the liver and heart into small pieces, add to the pan and fry till brown. Add the pine nuts, raisins, cracked cardamom pods and rice, and stir well. Add salt and pepper to taste, cinnamon and $2\frac{1}{2}$ cups of water, measured in the same cup as the rice. Bring to the boil, lower the heat to a gentle simmer and cover the pan. Cook for about 20 minutes without lifting the lid.
3   Check to see if the rice is cooked. If it is, all the water will have been absorbed and there will be little holes all over the surface. Leave to rest, covered, off the heat for a few minutes before serving.

Rice dishes form the basis of Iranian cuisine. ABOVE Rice fields in the foothills of the Elborn mountains.

RICE AND BROAD BEANS

PREPARATION TIME
50 minutes, including 10–15
   minutes soaking and 35
   minutes cooking

3–4 spring onions
15 ml [1 tbsp] oil
45 ml [3 tbsp] chopped fresh
   coriander
230–280 g [8–10 oz] frozen
   broad beans
salt and pepper to taste
5 ml [1 tsp] ground allspice
   (optional)
1 large teacupful long grain
   rice (about 230 g [8 oz], but
   measure by volume)
2 large teacupfuls water

(picture on page 102)

I usually keep a packet of frozen broad beans in the freezer. Since they need neither thawing, nor peeling because they are young, unlike most fresh ones, they are handy for a variety of quick dishes such as this one.

1 Cut the spring onions into 3 cm [1 in.] lengths and put them in a heavy-based pan with the oil and half the chopped coriander leaves. Set over medium heat. Add the broad beans straight from the freezer, salt, pepper and ground allspice if you like. Cover and leave to cook for 10 to 15 minutes, shaking the pan from time to time. Meanwhile wash the rice and leave it to soak.

2 When the beans are cooked there should be hardly any liquid left. Drain the rice and add to the pan. Add the rest of the chopped coriander and about 2 teacupfuls of water, measured in the same cup as you used for the rice, which should cover the ingredients to a depth of about 3 cm [1 in.]. Bring to the boil, then lower the heat and simmer, covered, for 20 minutes without lifting the lid. When the rice is cooked, let it rest for a few minutes before serving.

PERSIAN RICE WITH A CRUST

PREPARATION TIME
2 hours soaking (optional)
45 minutes, including 35
  minutes cooking

230 g [8 oz] basmati or Patna
  rice
salt to taste
60–80 g [2–3 oz] butter
1 egg yolk (optional)

(picture on page 103)

This is the second method of cooking rice that I find successful; one advantage is that there is no need to measure the water. However, the first few times you cook this rice, you might not succeed in getting a whole crust. At least you will get loose crusty grains, and the rice will be delicious anyway. It is also possible to make a crust without using an egg yolk.

1 Wash the rice until the water runs clear and leave to soak for a couple of hours if you have time.

2 Put plenty of water in a large, heavy-based, preferably non-stick saucepan and bring to the boil. Drain the rice and tip it into the boiling water, add salt and boil, uncovered, for about 4 minutes or until the grains are cooked through but not soft or soggy. Drain the rice, reserving a couple of tablespoonfuls of water in the pan.

3 Chop half the butter into small pieces and add to the pan with the egg yolk. Return just enough of the rice to cover the base. Mix all thoroughly and spread the rice out evenly by tapping the sides of the pan. Then add the rest of the rice and dot with the remaining butter. Tap again to level the rice, then cover the pan with a clean tea towel and replace the lid tightly over it. (If you don't have time to wait for a crust to form, rice cooked in this way is actually ready to eat a few minutes after returning it to the pan.) Set the pan over a medium heat, on a heat diffuser if you have one, making sure that the towel is folded up so that it does not catch fire. After about 15 minutes turn the heat down to low and cook for another 15 minutes or until the crust is formed.

4 Plunge the pan into cold water, remove the lid and leave for a few seconds or until the crust is freed from the bottom of the pan. Immediately spoon out the rice from above the crust on to the serving dish, then lift out the crust and pull or cut it into pieces. Serve these on a separate plate, or arrange around the rest of the rice, for people to munch throughout the meal.

Rice cooked in this way often incorporates other cooked ingredients: meat, poultry or vegetables. These are added at step 3, sandwiched between 2 layers of rice.

You can have a different, but equally delicious, crust by omitting the egg yolk. Simply mix half the butter (or if you prefer a mixture of butter and oil) with enough of the rice to just cover the base of the pan and continue as above.

A non-stick cake tin, generously buttered, can also be used. Put the tin, well-covered with foil so that it does not dry out, in a hot oven for 30–45 minutes. You should be able to turn it out on a plate like a cake with a crusty surface.

FILLET OF LAMB COOKED WITH RICE AND MILK

PREPARATION TIME
2 hours soaking (optional)
1 hour 15 minutes, including 1
  hour cooking

340 g [12 oz] short grain rice
450 g [1 lb] fillet of lamb
85 g [3 oz] butter
5–6 cracked cardamom pods
1.5 ml [¼ tsp] crushed mastic
5 ml [1 tsp] salt
570 ml [1 pint] milk

(picture on page 103)

Years after I left Egypt I was introduced to this unusual but very simple dish from the countryside. Although I have given exact weights for all the ingredients, they should be measured by volume, as I have explained below, using a 1.7 litre [3 pint] soufflé dish. The rice, lamb and milk should come only two-thirds of the way up the dish, to allow for rising. This way of measuring is also most useful if you want to vary the quantities.

To me, the success of this dish comes from the special, delicate aroma of the cardamom and mastic, blended with the rice, milk and lamb.

1 Take a soufflé dish and pour in dry, unwashed rice until it just covers the top joint of your thumb – make sure it is evenly spread. Remove the rice, wash it and soak in plenty of water for at least 2 hours.

2 Preheat the oven to 180°C [350°F, gas 4]. Cut the meat into slices about 1 cm [⅜ in.] thick. Butter the soufflé dish generously, not forgetting the sides.

3 Drain the rice and put half of it in the dish. Tap the dish to make sure that the rice is evenly distributed. Spread the pieces of meat over it, dot with the rest of the butter, sprinkle with the cardamom and mastic, and top with the rest of the rice. Sprinkle with a teaspoonful of salt and pour on milk slowly until it covers the rice to the depth of the top joint of your thumb. Put the dish in the oven for 1 hour or until it is puffed up with a beautiful golden crust.

POURGOURI PILAFI (BURGHUL PILAF)

PREPARATION TIME
30 minutes, including 20
    minutes cooking

1 teacupful (about 230 g [8 oz])
    burghul
30 ml [2 tbsp] olive oil
about 60 g [2 oz] vermicelli
1½ teacupfuls stock or water
salt to taste

(picture on page 76)

1 Rinse the burghul in a bowl of water, removing any chaff which floats to the surface. Tip it into a cloth and squeeze hard to remove most of the water.

2 Line the bottom of a heavy-based saucepan with olive oil and set over medium heat. Crush the vermicelli and fry it, stirring frequently, until golden brown. Take care not to burn it. Add the burghul and mix well. Add the stock or water and salt to taste. Bring to the boil, then lower the heat to simmer. Cover the pan and cook for about 20 minutes. When the pilaf is done, there will be little holes all over the surface.

3 Stretch a cloth over the top of the pan, replace the lid and leave off the heat for a few minutes before serving in the same way as rice.

VERMICELLI can be cooked in the same way on its own. Just brown it in oil or clarified butter, barely cover with water or stock and bring to the boil. Lower the heat and simmer, covered, for 4 or 5 minutes.

Rice can also be cooked in the same way.

BURGHUL PILAF WITH AUBERGINE AND CHEESE

PREPARATION TIME
30 minutes in salt
20 minutes, including cooking

1 medium aubergine
salt
1 teacupful (about 230 g [8 oz])
    burghul
30 ml [2 tbsp] oil
1 teacupful water
80–120 g [3–4 oz] cheese:
    halumi, mozzarella or mild
    Cheddar

(picture on page 102)

One of the best cooks I know, Mrs Lucie Farhi, taught me this unexpectedly delightful dish.

1 Cut the aubergine into 3 cm [1 in.] cubes. Put them in a colander, sprinkle with salt and leave to drain for at least 30 minutes. Meanwhile, wash the burghul and drain immediately.

2 Pat the aubergine dry with kitchen paper and fry it for a few minutes in the oil. With a slotted spoon, transfer the cubes into a sieve to let the oil run off. If you are using the same pan to cook the burghul, pour away the oil.

3 Tip the burghul into the pan, add a teacupful of water (measured with the same cup as the burghul) and simmer, covered, for about 5 minutes. Then add the aubergines, mix them in gently with a metal spoon, cover and return to the heat for a few more minutes. Then test to see if the burghul is tender.

4 When the burghul is done, cut the cheese into small cubes and add. Leave the pan covered, off the heat, until ready to serve.

The summer wheat harvest in North Yemen. Burghul, or cracked wheat, is made by washing and picking over the grain, then allowing it to dry and harden before it is stone ground to the required size.

COUSCOUS

PREPARATION TIME
1 hour 15 minutes, including 1
   hour 10 minutes cooking

SERVES 6

a 450 or 500 g [1 lb or 1lb 3oz]
   packet couscous
salt

(picture on page 83)

This traditional North African food is basically semolina. It is cooked in a 'couscoussière', a special two-part steamer with very small perforations in the base of the upper part. You can also use an ordinary steamer with a layer of muslin in the top to stop the grains of couscous falling through the larger holes. Preparation is simplicity itself, thanks to modern pre-processed couscous. Before this product was introduced, preparing couscous was a long and tricky business. Even pre-processed couscous is normally cooked in two stages, the first of which can conveniently be done in advance. Here is a successful and easy method for one standard-sized packet, either 450 or 500 g [1 lb or 1 lb 3 oz], which feeds about 6. I usually make more than I need and store the couscous and the stew to go with it in the freezer. They can both be reheated by steaming straight from the freezer.

1 Empty the couscous into a large bowl. Cover with cold water and immediately drain through a sieve. Turn the couscous out on to a large tray, spreading it out with the palms of your hands and rubbing it to keep it from forming lumps. Leave for about 20 minutes, sprinkling it with water and rubbing it from time to time.
2 Fill the bottom part of the steamer with water and set the top in place, making sure that it fits tightly. Bring the water to the boil: no steam should escape around the join. Put a shallow layer of couscous in the top of the steamer over boiling water. When the steam rises through the couscous, add the rest of the grains and sprinkle with salt. Steam uncovered for about 30 minutes.
3 Remove the steamer from the heat, carefully take off the top and turn the couscous out on to the tray. Again rub out the lumps. Sprinkle the couscous with a couple of teacupfuls of cold water, rub out the lumps again and leave it till you need it.
4 The second steaming is done in the same way except that you steam the couscous over the stew with which it is to be eaten, and only 20 minutes steaming is needed. Before you put the couscous in the steamer, rub out the lumps again. Fluff the couscous up with a fork from time to time. It can then be tipped straight from the detached top of the steamer into the serving dish.

QUICK COUSCOUS

PREPARATION TIME
35 minutes, including 25
   minutes cooking

1 small onion
30 ml [2 tbsp] oil
1 teacupful couscous
1 teacupful water
salt to taste

Some people – though certainly not North Africans – cook couscous like the rice for pilaf. It is a quick and simple method, but it does not give the lightness that real connoisseurs demand.

1 Finely chop the onion and gently sauté in oil until transparent, then add the couscous and water. Add salt and stir well. Bring to the boil, lower the heat and simmer, covered, without touching for 15 minutes.
2 Uncover the pan and see if the couscous is done. If it is, it will have absorbed all the water and the surface will be pitted with holes. Cook, covered, for a couple more minutes if necessary. Then stir, put a cloth over the pan, replace the lid and leave off the heat for 10 minutes. Serve as you would rice.

The various kinds of rice, grains and pasta commonly used in Middle Eastern cooking:
1 Brown rice 2 White rice 3 Whole wheat 4 Orzo ('birds' tongues': small pasta grains) 5 Coarse burghul 6 Penne 7 Tiny pasta for soups 8 Couscous 9 Fine burghul 10 Pasta shells 11 Pasta bows 12 Rigatoni 13 Macaroni 14 Vermicelli

KIBBEH

I only started making this burghul-based Lebanese and Syrian delicacy (which, incidentally, is also found in Cyprus) when I acquired a food processor. Traditionally, the burghul was pounded into a paste after soaking. Even using a mincer with a fine disc, this is a tedious job only worth undertaking for a dish of which one is very fond. A food processor reduces the work to a minimum and gives excellent results.

Kibbeh come in two forms, either baked in a tray or deep fried. The first is the simpler to make: the filling is sandwiched between two layers of shell mixture, then cut into rectangles or diamonds after baking. The second consists of meat-filled shells of varying shapes – from torpedoes to rounded ovals with pointed ends – depending on the individual cook.

Shell

1 Wash the burghul and soak for a few minutes in a bowl of water. Meanwhile, grate the onion in the food processor, add the meat in pieces and reduce to a smooth paste.

2 Drain the burghul in a muslin cloth and squeeze dry. Add it a little at a time to the running processor. Then add the flour if you are using it (though not essential, it does help to bind the mixture) and seasoning. The mixture should eventually be like a dough. Leave it in the refrigerator, uncovered, for about 1 hour before using.

Filling

3 Grate the onion and put it in a heavy-based frying pan with the minced meat, a little oil, ½ teacupful of water and the seasoning. Set over medium heat, break the mince up and turn it over, mix in the chopped parsley and cook half covered for 20 to 30 minutes.

4 When the meat is cooked and the whole mixture soft, add the nuts and raise the heat to brown the mixture. Transfer to a bowl to cool, then taste and adjust the seasoning.

Baked Kibbeh

5 Assemble the kibbeh. If baking the dish, knead the shell mixture with your hands (see page 77). Dampen your hands with cold water whenever the mixture begins to stick to them. Preheat the oven to 180°C [350°F, gas 4].

6 Butter a 20 cm [8 in.] square baking dish (not non-stick; it would get scratched) and line it with half the shell mixture about 1.5 cm [½ in.] thick, pressing down to get an even surface. Spread the filling mixture over it, then spread the rest of the shell mixture over the top. To avoid disturbing the filling when you even up this top layer, add it a little at a time and smooth the pieces together with dampened hands. Use a sharp knife with a wet blade to cut the mixture right through to the bottom into 5 cm [2 in.] diamonds or rectangles. Pour melted butter over the top. Bake for 45 minutes to 1 hour, or until brown. Serve warm or cold.

PREPARATION TIME FOR BAKED
   KIBBEH
**3 hours 10–40 minutes,
including 1 hour resting and
1 hour 10 minutes–1 hour
40 minutes cooking**

PREPARATION TIME FOR FRIED
   KIBBEH
**3 hours 15–35 minutes,
including 2 hours resting
and 35–55 minutes cooking**

SHELL
**230 g [8 oz] fine or medium
  burghul
1 small onion
120 g [4 oz] lean lamb
15 ml [1 tbsp] flour (optional)
salt and pepper to taste
5 ml [1 tsp] ground allspice**

FILLING
**1 medium onion
350 g [12 oz] minced lamb or
  beef, or a mixture of the two
15 ml [1 tbsp] oil
½ teacupful water
salt and pepper to taste
5 ml [1 tsp] ground allspice
5 ml [1 tsp] ground cinnamon
45 ml [3 tbsp] chopped parsley
30 ml [2 tbsp] pine nuts or
  coarsely chopped walnuts**

**30 g [1 oz] butter (for baked
  kibbeh) or oil for deep frying
  (for fried kibbeh)**

SHAPING AND FILLING KIBBEH FOR DEEP FRYING

Always keep a bowl of cold water handy, and moisten your hands whenever necessary.

1 Take an egg-sized piece of shell mixture, knead thoroughly and form into a smooth round ball, then shape it into an oval.

2 With your wet forefinger, gradually bore a hole in the centre of the oval, turning the kibbeh as you work the shell up your finger, pressing against your other hand. The shell should be as thin as possible.

3 Fill the shell with the meat mixture, and pinch with wet fingers to seal the end. If any cracks appear, smooth them out with wet fingers.

4 Roll the finished kibbeh in the palms of your hands to perfect the shape.

There are two ways of cooking Kibbeh: frying (*left*) and baking in a tray

Fried Kibbeh

5 If frying the kibbeh, have the shell and filling mixtures ready on your work surface, and a bowl of cold water with an ice cube in it.

6 Dampen your hands slightly with the iced water. Follow the step-by-step instructions above. Take an egg-sized piece of shell mixture and knead it well to make a round, even ball. Redampen your hands whenever it starts to stick to them. Shape the ball into an oval. Wet your forefinger and bore it gradually into the oval from one end, pressing against the palm of your other hand and turning and squeezing it with your fingers. Work the dough up your forefinger to make a long, hollow torpedo shape, squeezing the shell as thin as you can (the more experienced you get, the thinner the result will be). Spoon in the filling mixture and seal the end, using wetted fingers to smooth closed any cracks. Put each completed kibbeh on a plate. Leave them in the refrigerator or a cool dry place for about 1 hour before frying.

7 Deep fry until golden brown. They are delicious with Tahina Dip (see page 16).

Kibbeh shells can also be made with very lean beef, or without any meat at all, or with any proportion of meat to burghul; with experience, you can vary the quantities as you like. However, it is advisable for beginners to follow the recipe given above, especially if the mixture is to be formed into torpedoes, filled and fried, as it is easier to handle.

MATZO MEAL AND RICE FLOUR SHELL Another meatless, very light and crisp shell for fried kibbeh, made for me by Sonia Cohen. Use $\frac{3}{4}$ teacupful of matzo meal and $\frac{1}{4}$ teacupful of rice flour, seasoned with salt, pepper and 5 ml [1 tsp] ground allspice. Mix to a firm dough by gradually adding cold water: a food processor is useful for this. Fill and fry by the method given above.

KIBBEH NAYE Literally 'raw kibbeh', this dish is rather like steak tartare. It is made with a mixture of top-quality, very lean lamb and a small amount of burghul (about 6 parts lamb to 1 part burghul). Process together with a small onion and season with salt, pepper and allspice. Flatten the mixture on a small tray and serve with a little olive oil dribbled over the top.

Baked Macaroni and Ferik

BAKED MACARONI

PREPARATION TIME
1 hour 10–25 minutes,
   including 50 minutes–1
   hour 5 minutes cooking

500 g [1 lb] long, thick
   macaroni
salt
1 recipe Meat and Tomato
   Sauce (see page 137)
1.2 litres [2 pints] Béchamel
   Sauce (see page 138)
2 eggs
120 g [4 oz] grated cheese: a
   mixture of Emmenthal with
   mature Cheddar or
   Parmesan

Pasta of many different shapes and forms, both fresh and dried, is popular all over the Middle East. The small kinds are added to soups. Others are cooked in broth, or boiled in plain water, and served with sauces made from the cooking liquid from braised chicken or meat. Baked macaroni dishes are particular favourites, made at home or bought from takeaway shops or street stalls. This was one of my mother's specialities.

1 Cook the macaroni in a large pan with plenty of fast-boiling, salted water. The pan should be large enough for the macaroni to swim freely in: this is one of the secrets of good pasta cooking. After about 15 minutes test it by biting a piece. It should be just tender. Drain it and put in a large bowl with the Meat and Tomato Sauce and a couple of tablespoonfuls of the Béchamel. Mix well.

2 Preheat the oven to 200°C [400°F, gas 6]. Transfer the mixture to an ovenproof dish. Beat the eggs into the rest of the Béchamel Sauce, which should be allowed to cool a little if just made, or the eggs will curdle. Pour over the macaroni and top with the grated cheese. Bake for 30 to 45 minutes, until golden on top. Cut into squares to serve.

BAKED MACARONI WITH AUBERGINES Slices of fried aubergine, some added to the macaroni mixture and others laid on top before pouring on the Béchamel Sauce, make a delicious addition to this dish. Sprinkle the aubergine slices with salt and leave overnight (see page 21) before frying, to reduce the amount of oil they take up.

MOUSSAKA I make Moussaka, the classic Greek dish, in the same way, using more fried aubergine slices instead of the macaroni layered with the meat and Béchamel Sauce and ending with Béchamel Sauce.

FERIK

PREPARATION TIME
Soaking time 10 minutes
45 minutes (or 2 hours 15
   minutes), including 30
   minutes in pressure cooker
   (or 2 hours in a saucepan)

250 g [or 8 oz] whole wheat
1 large onion
500 g [or 1 lb] veal knuckle
   (weight without bone)
marrow bone pieces (optional)
about 30 ml [2 tbsp] oil
4 eggs
salt and pepper to taste

TO SERVE
salt, pepper and ground cumin

Wheat, man's oldest
cultivated crop, was first
domesticated in the Middle
East. Much of the grain is
ground into flour, but the
whole grain is also cooked
(see above and page 122) or
boiled whole with sour milk
and dried to make *kischk* (see
pages 43, 60 and 136).
BELOW Sacks of grain being
loaded on to an oxen-drawn
cart during the Turkish
wheat harvest.

This hearty dish is usually made in the Middle East with green, not quite ripe wheat; but ordinary, dry whole wheat is perfectly adequate. Use a pressure cooker, as described here, to save long cooking. If you don't have one, a large, heavy-based saucepan will do. Simply multiply the cooking times for the pressure cooker by 4. The pressure cooker should be a fairly large one, which the ingredients only half fill, since the wheat will swell quite a bit. Alternatively, you could take the opposite course and cook the dish in an electric slow cooker, which will take several hours. Veal knuckle is ideal for slow-cooking dishes of this type. Ask your butcher to bone it and give you a couple of pieces of marrow bone for extra flavour.

1 Wash the wheat well and soak it in water for at least 10 minutes.
2 Finely chop the onion and cut the meat into chunks. Pour enough oil into the base of the pressure cooker to coat it, and set over medium heat. Brown the meat, remove and set aside; then lower the heat, add the onion and cook until soft. Increase the heat to brown the onion, then return the meat to the pan. Add the bones if you have them.
3 Drain the wheat and add it to the pan. Add enough water to cover the wheat by 5 cm [2 in.]. Put in the eggs in their shells. Close the lid, bring up the pressure and cook for 20 minutes. At the end of this time the meat should be tender enough to cut with a fork, and the wheat swollen and burst. Add salt and pepper.
4 Serve in a deep bowl or tureen, leaving the eggs unpeeled and providing dishes of salt, pepper and ground cumin. Each person peels an egg and dips it in the condiments. The whites will have turned brown and the yolks a creamy ochre, and they will have a special, delicate flavour.

Ferik is also often cooked with shin of beef or cow's or calf's feet, in the same way as the haricot beans on page 98.

For a vegetarian dish, cook as above but without the meat, and add another medium onion. Fry the onions until soft, then increase the heat and cook until dark brown. This gives the dish a delicious flavour, and the eggs make it a rich and nutritious meal.

For added flavour, a Ta'leya (see page 140) made by frying thin slices of onion and crushed coriander seed can be added just before serving.

SWEET DISHES & BREADS

The most common dessert in the Middle East is fruit. The region produces an extraordinary variety: citrus fruit, grapes, melons and watermelons, apricots, dates, figs, mangoes and guavas, among others. The best dried fruits also come from this area, and form the basis of numerous sweet meats and desserts. Dried dates and figs are often served after a meal, with a mixture of nuts, and nibbled throughout the evening, in much the same way as they are eaten in Britain at Christmas time.

Other sweet dishes are also common throughout the region. Almost everywhere one finds puddings made with rice or rice flour and milk or water, flavoured with rose or orange flower water and often mastic, and usually served cold. These are often eaten for breakfast as well as at the end of a meal. All kinds of ice cream are very popular, and it is hardly surprising to find an enormous variety of fruit ices, which vary according to season. But perhaps the chief glory of the region is its pastries. All kinds of small delicacies, stuffed with nuts and dried fruits, are enjoyed with coffee at any time of the day.

Three delicious fruit desserts (*left to right*) Pomegranates in Lime and Rosewater Syrup, Date and Banana Dessert and Guavas in Lime Juice

GUAVAS IN LIME JUICE

PREPARATION TIME
10 minutes
30 minutes wait

juice of 1–2 limes
30–45 ml [2–3 tbsp] **sugar, or to taste**
4 guavas

(picture on page 114)

The fragrance of guavas macerating in lime juice and sugar always reminds me of my childhood. When I came home from school at lunchtime it wafted over me the moment I opened the door. My mother used to prepare guavas in this way as soon as they were in season.

1 Mix the lime juice and sugar in a bowl and stir until the sugar dissolves. Guavas, like bananas or pears, turn brown as soon as they are peeled, so prepare them one at a time and put the flesh straight into the lime juice. Peel each one, cut it in half, scoop out the soft centre with the seeds and reserve it, then slice the rest and turn it over in the lime juice to coat it well. Prepare the remaining guavas in the same way and put the bowl in the refrigerator.

2 Press the centres through a nylon sieve to remove the pulp from the pips (or use a food processor). Add the pulp to the bowl. Taste, and adjust the flavouring. Leave in the refrigerator until the time of serving.

POMEGRANATES IN LIME AND ROSEWATER SYRUP

PREPARATION TIME
10 minutes
2–3 hours wait

2 pomegranates
100 g [3½ oz] **sugar, or to taste**
1 teacupful water
juice of 1 lime
15 ml [1 tbsp] **rose water**

(picture on page 114)

The pretty, transparent ruby pulp enclosing pomegranate seeds makes a very refreshing dessert.

1 Cut the fruit in half and carefully remove the seeds in their transparent coats, discarding the whitish membrane to which they are attached. This can be a little tricky: take care not to squash them.

2 Dissolve the sugar completely in a teacupful of water. Put the seeds in a bowl with this syrup and the lime juice. Mix well and add the rose water. Leave in the refrigerator for a few hours. Before serving, taste and add more rose water if needed. Serve in individual bowls.

DATE AND BANANA DESSERT

PREPARATION TIME
30 minutes
2 hours wait

SERVES 8–10

450 g [1 lb] **fresh dates, or** 300 g [11 oz] **dried dates**
450 g [1 lb] **bananas**
280 ml [10 fl oz] **double cream**

(picture on page 114)

I first went back to Egypt in the mid 1950s, six years after my family had emigrated. Everywhere I went I was offered this 'new' dessert which I loved. So did my Egyptian friends in London when I made it for them after my return. Use fresh dates if you can: they are quite easy to find these days. Dried dates are a good substitute as long as they are not old and withered, so examine them carefully before you buy.

1 Wash the fresh dates one at a time in a large bowl full of water. Peel each one if using fresh dates; dried dates do not need washing or peeling. If you are not used to peeling fresh dates, this is how to do it. You will need to keep your hands and the knife blade wet while you peel and stone them. Cut off each end with a sharp knife, then make a shallow cut around the middle of the date, just through the skin. Hold the date with the thumb and two fingers of each hand on either side of the cut, and twist the two halves of the skin. It should come off quite easily as long as the date is ripe. Split the date open lengthways so that you can remove the stone, but don't completely halve it. Lay the split dates in a serving bowl until the bottom is covered in a single layer.

2 Peel and slice some of the bananas to make a layer on top of the dates, and pour on some of the cream to stop them from turning black. Then add more dates, more bananas and cream and so on, finishing with a layer of dates. Pour on the last of the cream to coat the dates evenly. Leave in the refrigerator for at least 2 hours before serving.

To make an even richer dessert you can add a few roughly chopped walnuts or roasted almonds.

Oranges, lemons and limes on sale in the orange market at Hammamet in eastern Tunisia.

KHOCHAF

PREPARATION TIME
15 minutes
3 days soaking

FOR SEVERAL DAYS' SERVINGS

120 g [4 oz] raisins
120 g [4 oz] sultanas
120 g [4 oz] dried peaches
230 g [8 oz] dried apricots
230–280 g [8–10 oz] prunes
a piece of *amardine* **(apricot paste) roughly 10 cm [4 in] square (optional)**

TO SERVE (optional)
a few roasted almonds, walnuts, pistachios or hazelnuts, coarsely chopped
rose or orange flower water

(picture on page 118)

The recipe for this dried fruit salad makes quite a large quantity since you have to use a certain amount of each of the dried fruits, and they swell tremendously as they soak up water. However, it keeps very well in the refrigerator, and in fact even improves with longer soaking than the three days recommended here. A vegetarian friend of mine has even adopted it as his favourite breakfast. Nuts and flavouring are added just before serving. The addition of 'amardine' (an apricot paste available in Middle Eastern shops) to the salad improves it tremendously; if you cannot get it add more dried apricots instead.

1 Cut the larger fruit (anything bigger than a small prune) into a few pieces, but leave the rest whole. Cut the *amardine* into 1 cm [$\frac{3}{8}$ in.] squares with scissors, wetting the blades if they stick. Put this with the fruit into the largest bowl you can fit into your refrigerator, to allow the contents to swell. Cover the fruit with at least 5 cm [2 in.] of water.

2 Leave in the refrigerator for 3 days. Stir it well from time to time and add more water as necessary to keep the fruit covered. It is superb served just as it is, or with one of the following additions sprinkled on just before serving.

Roast, coarsely chopped almonds, walnuts, pistachios or hazelnuts, or a mixture, give a crunchy contrast in texture as well as added flavour. A sprinkling of rose or orange flower water lends a light freshness to this rather rich dessert.

FRUITS

In the Middle East, fresh fruit is so varied, plentiful and cheap that it not only features regularly at the end of every meal, but is also eaten at all times of the day. Freshly squeezed fruit juices of every kind – from mango and orange to guava, apricot and sugar cane juice – are sold on street corners everywhere.

Fruit is often part of a light evening meal on a hot summer evening: one of my favourite combinations is iced watermelon and feta cheese. Oranges and grapes also go very well with feta cheese, and bananas are nice with *kashkaval*, a goat's cheese similar in texture to a good mature Cheddar – which, incidentally, also goes surprisingly well with bananas.

A fresh fruit salad has always been my favourite dessert. In my family, it was usually a simple combination of oranges, bananas and strawberries with orange or lime juice. In the following recipe, substitute any fruit you like, remembering that exotic fruit makes it special.

FRESH FRUIT SALAD

Now that a good range of tropical and subtropical fruits are available in Britain at most times of the year, I often make a fruit salad with whatever is available, supplemented by good local fruit – fresh, never canned – such as apples, pears and strawberries, if a large quantity is required. To serve 8–10 people, peel and slice some or all of the following: a medium-sized ripe melon, a mango, a small papaya, $\frac{1}{2}$ pineapple, 2 or 3 guavas, and mix in a bowl with the juice of a lime (or lemon) and 1 or 2 oranges (or a teacupful of mixed tropical fruit juice). I never add sugar as I find the sweetness of the fruit is adequate.
* The salad may be prepared in advance to this stage, and kept in the refrigerator.

Peel, slice and add 2 bananas at the last moment, mix in well and serve.

The richly varied fruits of the Middle East:
1 Mangoes 2 Limes 3 Papaya
4 Fresh Fruit Salad 5 Kumquats
6 Khochaf, a rich dried fruit
salad 7 Persimmons 8 Figs
9 Pomegranates

ICES

Countless people from all over the world who served in Egypt during the Second World War have fond memories of Groppi's, which we proudly called the best *patisserie* in the world. A Swiss firm, it excelled in ices. As soon as the mango season started, we used to rush there from school for a daily mango sorbet; their strawberry, apricot and pistachio ices were just as tempting. However, I came to consider that by far the best ice cream was to be had at a popular café whose Yugoslav owner specialized in Dondurma Kaymak – simply the Turkish for ice cream. It was snow-white, with a most distinctive flavour of mastic and an astonishingly elastic texture – almost like melted Gruyère! The essential ingredients for this delicacy were milk, cream and sugar, mastic of course, and a thickener called *sahleb*, made from the root of an orchid.

DONDURMA KAYMAK

PREPARATION TIME
30–45 minutes, including cooking
about 13 hours freezing

8 ml [1 heaped tsp] **arrowroot**
1 litre [1¾ pints] **milk**
170 g [6 oz] **vanilla sugar**
1.5 ml [¼ tsp] **crushed mastic**
280 ml [10 fl oz] **double cream**

During our first years in Britain, in the early 1950s, my aunt sent me a recipe for this much-loved ice cream, giving cornflour as a substitute for 'sahleb', which she was sure was unobtainable here. Little did she realize that in rationed post-war Britain, cream was just as scarce! Now you might find 'sahleb', under its Greek name of 'salep', which is also the usual English term, at some Greek food stores. I find that arrowroot is a much better substitute than cornflour.

1 Dissolve the arrowroot in about a teacupful of the milk in a heavy-based saucepan and start cooking on a low heat, stirring all the time. When it begins to thicken, take it off the heat and beat vigorously until you get a smooth paste. Add another ½ teacupful of milk, stir until even, return to the heat and keep stirring and adding milk until you have used most of it. This should take a good 20 minutes in all. Then add the vanilla sugar and the last of the milk, stir to dissolve the sugar completely and cook on a low heat, stirring continuously.

2 Add the crushed mastic to the mixture, then the cream, and begin stirring again while you increase the heat to medium. Bring the mixture to the boil, making sure that your spoon reaches every part of the bottom and sides of the pan to avoid any sticking. Boil for about 1 minute, still stirring, then pour the mixture into a heatproof bowl and let it cool.

3 When the mixture is completely cold, taste and adjust the flavouring if necessary. Put it in the freezer for about 1 hour, until it becomes slushy. Then take it out and beat vigorously (in a food processor or liquidizer if you have one).

4 Return the mixture to the freezer for 30 minutes, then take it out and beat it again. Return and beat 3 or 4 times at 30 minute intervals. After the last beating, pour the mixture into a mould, cover and freeze for about 10 hours. Transfer it from the freezer to the refrigerator about 20 minutes before you want to eat it. The flavour is as good as I ever remember it, though the texture and colour are not quite the same.

Huge bunches of dates drying in sun on a fruit stall in Jericho. Dates, figs and apricots are often dried together in Middle Eastern homes, hanging in bunches from the ceiling. In Islamic countries dates are one of the holy foods with which Moslems may break their daylight fast during the month of Ramadan.

The contrasting flavours and textures of creamy Dondurma Kaymak and Mango Ice combine to make a delicious dessert

MANGO ICE

PREPARATION TIME
10 minutes, including cooking
about 15 hours freezing

1 400 g [14 oz] can 'Alfonso'
    type mangoes or mango pulp
15 ml [1 tbsp] sugar (optional)
juice of 1 lime or lemon

A food processor or liquidizer is more or less essential for this recipe. The canned mangoes must be either Indian or Egyptian – of the 'Alfonso' type. I make fresh fruit ices with 230 g [8 oz] of fruit to a syrup made with 120 g [4 oz] of sugar and 570 ml [10 fl oz] water, and with the juice of a lime or lemon, and with dried fruits such as apricots I use the water which the fruit has soaked in instead of syrup. However, since for this mango ice I use canned fruit, which is already sweetened, you will find that you need only a little more sugar, if any, and no water.

1 Liquidize the mangoes with their juice if necessary. Put in a pan with the sugar (if used) and lime juice, bring to the boil and stir for 3 or 4 minutes. Transfer to a heatproof bowl and leave until completely cold. Beat for 1 minute in the food processor, then return to the bowl and put in the freezer for about 1 hour.

2 Process the mixture for another minute, then put it in the freezer for 30 minutes. Repeat this 3 or 4 times at 30 minute intervals. The more you do it, the creamier the final texture of the ice. Transfer the mixture to a mould, cover it and freeze for about 12 hours. About 20 minutes before you want to eat the ice, take it out of the freezer and put in the refrigerator.

COMBINED ICES Not only are Dondurma Kaymak and this mango water ice my favourite ices; they make an unmatchable combination. Use a mould which will take both together. Make the Mango Ice first, and start making the Dondurma Kaymak as soon as you have put the water ice into the freezer. After it has had 4 or 5 beatings and the cream ice 3 or 4, put the cream ice into the final mould. Give the water ice a last beating, then after 30 minutes in the freezer pour it into the mould on top of the cream ice, which should be stiff enough to keep the two separate. Freeze for 12 hours. To serve, plunge the mould almost to the rim into a large bowl of very hot water for a few seconds. Turn out on to a serving plate. Alternatively, you could make the two ices separately, one in a ring mould and the other in a pudding basin small enough to fit inside the ring, and unmould them so that one surrounds the other.

MEHALABEYA

PREPARATION TIME
**40–45 minutes, including
25–35 minutes cooking
1 hour cooling**

**75 ml [3 heaped tbsp] cornflour
1.5 litres [2½ pints] milk
45 ml [3 tbsp] sugar
15–30 ml [1–2 tbsp] orange
flower water
1 ml [⅛ tsp] crushed mastic**

TO GARNISH
ground cinnamon or nuts

There is a whole range of Middle Eastern milk or milk and water puddings thickened with cornflour, or ground or whole rice. The usual flavourings are rose or orange flower water, and cinnamon, mastic or vanilla, variously combined. Often they are enriched with pistachios, almonds or hazelnuts, and dried fruits such as raisins and sultanas.

1 Take a large, very heavy-based pan, or a large double boiler. Dissolve the cornflour in just enough of the cold milk to give a smooth, thin mixture and set the pan over a very low heat or, for a double boiler, a medium heat, stirring constantly. As soon as the mixture thickens, start stirring very vigorously, not neglecting the edges of the pan, while you gradually add about 1 litre [1¾ pints] of the milk.

2 Add the sugar, stir well and taste. If you can detect the taste of uncooked cornflour, carry on adding the rest of the milk gradually and stirring. If the uncooked taste has gone, you can add the milk more quickly. When all the milk has been added and the taste is satisfactory, raise the heat to medium – or high for a double boiler – and keep stirring while the mixture comes to the boil. Make sure that it doesn't stick anywhere. When the mixture attains a thick, creamy consistency, take it off the heat and add orange flower water and crushed mastic. Taste, bearing in mind that the flavouring will be stronger after it has had time to infuse and the mixture has cooled.

3 Pour the mixture into individual bowls and leave it in a cool place to set. It should have a pleasant jelly consistency, neither liquid nor rubbery. Refrigerate until ready to serve, then sprinkle with ground cinnamon or chopped nuts.

For a lighter, less rich pudding, replace some of the milk with water, in any proportions; or use skimmed milk.

BALOUZA is a version of this pudding made with water, and no milk at all. It is a beautifully delicate, translucent jelly.

Both Mehalabeya and Balouza can be made with ground or whole rice instead of cornflour. Here are a few ideas for different flavourings and additions; they should all be stirred into the mixture before it sets. Flavourings can include a few drops of real vanilla essence (or use vanilla sugar) instead of the mastic. This gives an equally delicious flavour more familiar to European tastes. You can also mix in shelled, whole or halved pistachios, pieces of roasted almonds, raisins or other nuts or fruit. I like to add chopped dried apricots, which contrast sharply with the creamy flavour. A usual Egyptian addition is a tablespoonful of Ashoura (see below), a wheat pudding, which gives an interesting texture.

ASHOURA

PREPARATION TIME
**10 minutes soaking
2 hours, including cooking
1 hour cooling**

FOR SEVERAL DAYS' SERVINGS

**about 500 g [or 1 lb] whole
wheat or barley**

TO SERVE
**milk
sugar
orange flower water
ground cinnamon**

This is made with either wheat or barley. The whole grains are simply boiled until they burst, and then eaten with milk and various flavourings. It is a surprisingly light but nourishing dish which is equally good as a dessert or for breakfast. It is worth while making a large quantity, as it takes a long time to cook and keeps extremely well in the refrigerator for a week or so. However, using a pressure cooker saves a lot of time.

1 Wash and rinse the wheat or barley thoroughly and leave it to soak in plenty of water for about 10 minutes. Drain, rinse again and put it in a pan or pressure cooker. Add water to cover the grain by about 3 cm [1 in.]. Cook for at least 2 hours, or 20 minutes in a pressure cooker, until the grain has swollen and burst. Transfer it to a bowl and leave to cool completely. When cold, the liquid should have the consistency of jelly.

2 Cover the bowl with cling film and keep it in the refrigerator. Dip in whenever you need it. Eat it in one of the ways described below.

Take a bowlful of Ashoura and add hot or cold milk and some sugar, according to taste. Then sprinkle on some additional flavouring such as ground cinnamon or a few drops of orange flower water. (If you overdo the flavouring, just mix in some more Ashoura and milk.) A tablespoonful of Ashoura is also often added to Mehalabeya or Balouza (see above).

Ashoura (*left*), served for breakfast or pudding with milk, sugar and perhaps cinnamon, Mehalabeya (*front right*) and Sutlach

SUTLACH

PREPARATION TIME
2½–3½ hours, including
   cooking
1 hour cooling

SERVES 8

80 g [3 oz] **ground rice**
2 litres [3½ pints] **milk**
15 ml [1 tbsp] **sugar**

CARAMEL
230 g [8 oz] **sugar**
45 ml [3 tbsp] **water** + a
   teacupful
a little lemon juice

Of all the puddings my mother used to make, this beautiful, brown-marbled dish was the most appreciated by the constant flow of my father's army colleagues who came to our table in Cairo during the Second World War. Essentially a rice pudding, it is enlivened by a caramel topping.

1 First make a ground rice pudding using the method for Mehalabeya (see opposite) with the ingredients given on the left. While the mixture is still hot, pour it into an ovenproof dish, preferably glass. The mixture should be no more than about 4 cm [1½ in.] deep in the dish. Preheat the oven to cool, 150°C [300°F, gas 2].

2 Make a caramel by dissolving the sugar in the water over a low heat. When the mixture is transparent add a squeeze of lemon juice. Increase the heat and cook until the syrup takes on a golden colour. Remove the pan from the heat and add a teacupful of cold water carefully, to avoid scalding splashes of the very hot syrup. Stir well, then trail over the top of the rice pudding.

3 Put the dish on the bottom shelf of the oven, reduce the heat to very cool, 120°C [250°F, gas ½] and leave to cook for 2 to 3 hours, until the topping bursts into bubbles and seeps down into the rice mixture. (If you have used an ovenproof glass dish you will be able to see that this has happened.) Allow to cool, then refrigerate until ready to serve. This pudding does not need any flavouring other than the caramel.

GHORAYEBA

PREPARATION TIME
50 minutes, including 30
   minutes wait and 20
   minutes cooking

60 g [2 oz] hazelnuts
240 g [8 oz] plain flour + more
   for baking tray
240 g [8 oz] butter + more for
   baking tray
120 g [4 oz] caster sugar
icing sugar

Also called 'ghorabi', this is at its simplest a rich short biscuit made with flour, butter and sugar roughly in the proportions 5:4:2. There are numerous variations in ingredients and flavourings, each of which has a distinctive character. My favourite is one with hazelnuts. I prefer to roast the nuts in a dry frying pan rather than blanch them. It is then easy to rub off most of the peel.

1 Roast the hazelnuts, peel them and grind them as finely as possible; but not so much that they become an oily paste. If you use a food processor to grind the nuts, put them in with a couple of tablespoonfuls of the flour. Sift the ground nuts together with the flour. Cream the butter and sugar together, then add the flour and nuts, mix well and knead until smooth. Leave in a cool place for at least 30 minutes while you prepare a baking tray by buttering it, sprinkling it with flour and shaking off the excess, and preheat the oven to moderate, 180°C [350°F, gas 4].

2 Damp your hands slightly with cold water (see page 77). Take a walnut-sized piece of the biscuit dough, knead it very well and form it into smooth balls, moistening your hands again at the slightest sign of sticking. Lay the balls on the baking tray, leaving plenty of space between them, damp your thumb and gently press it down into the centre of each one to make a small dent.

3 Bake for about 20 minutes. The biscuits should remain fairly white, and they will be very fragile, so don't take them off the tray until they are completely cool. Leave them for an hour or so to cool completely, sprinkle them with icing sugar, then store them in a biscuit tin.

Ghorayeba are sometimes made oblong, and sometimes the mixture is bound with an egg. But whatever shape or ingredients you choose, the final result may be unexpected until you have made them often enough in the same oven. Sometimes they go quite flat, which is why you need a lot of space between them on the tray, sometimes the shape changes very little. All this depends partly on some things you can control, such as the way you knead and roll the mixture – thorough kneading helps to make them firm – and some that you can't, such as the variable temperature of any oven, or differences in the flour, sugar or nuts. But whatever the shape, the taste is delicious. To vary the flavour, use ground almonds instead of hazelnuts, or moisten your hands with a touch of rose or orange flower water instead of plain water when rolling.

A street-vendor in Aleppo, Syria, selling honey-sweet cakes and pastries made from the huge round trays in which they are baked. The cakes may be made from semolina, flour or ground nuts: one of the most popular is an anise-flavoured bread sweetened with rosewater syrup.

Walnut Biscuits (*front*) and Ghorayeba, rich short biscuits

WALNUT BISCUITS

PREPARATION TIME
**25–30 minutes, including
1 5–20 minutes cooking**

MAKES 2 DOZEN BISCUITS

260 g [9 oz] **broken walnuts**
60 g [2 oz] **caster sugar**
2 egg whites

These biscuits are made without flour.

1 Reserve about 60 g [2 oz] of the largest pieces of walnut for decoration. Grind the rest to the consistency of coarse sand and mix them with sugar. Beat the egg whites, and mix in the ground nuts and sugar thoroughly.

2 Preheat the oven to moderate, 180°C [350°F, gas 4]. Lightly grease a baking tray. Have a bowl of cold water beside you, and moisten your hands as often as necessary (see page 77) while you knead the mixture well, then roll it into walnut-sized balls. There will be enough for a couple of dozen. Put them on the tray with a good space between them, and stick a piece of walnut on each. Bake for 15 to 20 minutes, until they are a nice dark golden colour.

MARONCHINOS are similar to these walnut biscuits. My grandmother used to make them, but with very finely ground almonds instead of coarsely ground walnuts.

Semolina and Date Cookies, Date Menenas and Pistachio Menenas

SEMOLINA AND DATE COOKIES

PREPARATION TIME
10 minutes, including 2–3
    minutes cooking
1 day drying

MAKES 2 DOZEN COOKIES

225 g [8 oz] stoned dates
50 g [2 oz] butter
125 g [generous 4 oz] coarse
    semolina

1 Finely chop the dates, mix with the butter and work into a paste in a food processor if you have one. This takes some time by hand, using a damp knife.

2 Dry roast the semolina in a heavy-based frying pan, preferably non-stick, stirring constantly. As soon as the semolina begins to colour and smell roasted, remove the pan from the heat, continuing to stir for a while. You can return the pan to a very low heat to get an even colour, but take care as it easily burns.

3 Mix the semolina and date paste thoroughly and spread the mixture a generous 1 cm [$\frac{1}{2}$ in.] thick over a sheet of foil or greaseproof paper. Use a sharp knife with a wetted blade to cut out 3 cm [1 in.] wide diamond shapes. There should be enough for about 2 dozen. Separate them, peeling off the foil, and leave to dry out in a cool place. The roasted semolina will be crunchy, contrasting pleasantly with the smoothness of the dates.

MENENAS

Also called *ma'moul*, this is another of the many rich pastries filled with fruit pastes or nuts. It is made in two ways: either the pastry and filling is rolled up like a miniature Swiss roll and cut into slices, or the pastry is made into a hollow ball and stuffed. I've cooked all kinds of versions, and the two following recipes are my favourites. The first is by Angèle Argi, a great friend of my late aunt, with whom she always exchanged recipes. She comes to my rescue whenever I want to re-create any of my aunt's favourite sweet dishes. Follow the step-by-step instructions below.

DATE MENENAS

PREPARATION TIME
2 hours to soften butter
2 hours, including 30 minutes cooling and 1 hour cooking

MAKES 2 DOZEN SLICES

DOUGH
90 g [3½ oz] butter
250 g [9 oz] plain flour
15 ml [1 tbsp] icing sugar
15 ml [1 tbsp] oil
30 ml [2 tbsp] milk

FILLING
230 g [8 oz] stoned dates
10 g [scant ½ oz] butter
30 ml [2 tbsp] water

icing sugar

1 Leave the butter out of the refrigerator for a couple of hours, or until it is quite soft.

2 Cut the butter into small pieces and work it into the flour to make fine, even crumbs. (A food processor makes this dough well.) Add the icing sugar and mix in thoroughly. Make a well in the centre of the mixture and pour in the oil and milk. Gradually mix it in until you get a dough which leaves the sides of the bowl clean. Knead it well for a good 10 minutes, then wrap it in cling film and put in the refrigerator.

3 Make the filling. First chop the dates finely, taking care to remove any stones that may be left. (If you are using a food processor, cut the block of dates into smallish pieces first so that you can find all the stones.) Put the dates in a heavy-based frying pan with the butter and a couple of tablespoonfuls of water. Set the pan over a low heat and let the mixture melt gently into a paste, stirring and pressing it from time to time. When it is ready, leave it to cool.

4 Grease and flour a baking sheet, shaking off the excess flour. Preheat the oven to moderate, 180°C [350°F, gas 4]. Take the pastry out of the refrigerator and cut it into three pieces. Knead each of them well and roll out as thinly as possible into a rectangle. Spread one-third of the paste on to one rectangle, leaving a good 1 cm [⅜ in.] border of uncovered pastry all round. Now roll up the rectangle from one end. When the roll is made, continue rolling it backwards and forwards, pressing down lightly to lengthen it. Slightly flatten the roll and slice it diagonally into pieces about 2 cm [¼ in.] thick. Put these on the baking sheet. Continue with the rest of the pastry and filling. You should end up with at least 2 dozen slices. Prick the tops lightly with a fork.

5 Bake for 20 to 30 minutes. The menenas should be white on top and slightly coloured underneath. Let them cool, then sprinkle with icing sugar.

SHAPING DATE MENENAS

1 Spread the date paste mixture thinly all over the rectangle of pastry, leaving a border of uncovered pastry all round the edge.

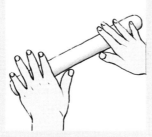

2 Roll up the pastry into a fairly thick sausage shape. Continue rolling it backwards and forwards, pressing down gently at the same time to make it thinner and longer.

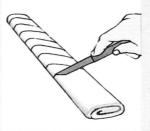

3 Flatten the roll slightly, then cut it diagonally into slices about 2cm (3/4 in.) thick.

4 Separate the slices and bake on a greased and floured sheet.

PISTACHIO MENENAS

PREPARATION TIME
2 hours to soften butter
1 hour 15 minutes, including
   30 minutes cooling and 30
   minutes cooking

MAKES 2 DOZEN BALLS

DOUGH
80 g [3 oz] butter
250 g [9 oz] plain flour
30 g [1 oz] icing sugar
5 ml [1 tsp] skimmed milk
   powder
2.5 ml [½ tsp] baking powder
45 ml [3 tbsp] oil
60 ml [3 tbsp] orange flower
   water

FILLING
120 g [4 oz] pistachio nuts
   (weight without shells)
30 g [1 oz] sugar
a little orange flower water

icing sugar

(picture on page 126)

This is another of Sonia Cohen's specialities with a most unexpected ingredient – dried skimmed milk powder – and this from someone who insists that Baklava can never be made with anything but pistachios or almonds, and that it is really beyond the pale to use hazelnuts or walnuts as I do. But I must admit that her menenas are the best I have ever tasted.

1 Let the butter soften at room temperature for a couple of hours.
2 Make the dough (in a food processor if you have one) as for Date Menenas (see page 127) using the ingredients here – but reserve half the orange flower water for a later stage. Refrigerate the dough. Meanwhile, gently roast and shell the pistachios, chop them fairly coarsely – but not too large or stuffing will be difficult – mix them with the sugar and lightly moisten them with orange flower water.
3 Lightly grease and flour a baking sheet, knocking off the excess flour. Preheat the oven to moderate, 180°C [350°F, gas 4]. Have a small bowl with a little orange flower water to moisten your hands, and keep moistening them lightly to prevent the dough from sticking. Take a piece of dough the size of a walnut, and knead it well to make a smooth ball. Moisten the tip of your index finger and make a hole in the ball. Insert a little filling and close up the ball. Roll it on your palm to restore its roundness, prick it lightly all over with a fork and put it on the baking sheet.
4 When all the balls are finished – there should be about 2 dozen – bake for about 20 minutes. They should not colour. Let them cool, then sprinkle with icing sugar. They keep well in a tin, but they must be quite cold before you put them in.

The recipe for the following filling was given to me by Emily Amiel, a lifelong family friend now living in Canada.

PUMPKIN FILLING Another delectable filling for menenas. Mix 250 g [8 oz] of diced pumpkin with 120 g [4 oz] of sugar and the juice of ½ lemon. Cook over a low heat, uncovered. At first liquid will exude from the pumpkin. Continue cooking gently until this has dried out. Flavour with cinnamon or, better still, a spot of crushed mastic.

APRICOT PETITS FOURS

PREPARATION TIME
2 hours 20 minutes, including
   20 minutes cooking and 1½
   hours cooling
2–3 days drying

MAKES 2 DOZEN PETITS FOURS

250 g [8 oz] dried apricots
120 g [4 oz] caster sugar
30 g [1 oz] butter
15 ml [1 tbsp] orange flower
   water + more for rolling
30 ml [2 tbsp] water
granulated sugar for rolling

These delectable fruit pastes are one of Sonia Cohen's specialities. They must be made in advance, a few days before they are needed, to give them time to dry out.

1 Chop the apricots very finely. Put them in a heavy-based frying pan with the caster sugar, butter, orange flower water and a couple of tablespoonfuls of water. Set over a medium heat. Cook, stirring from time to time, until the mixture has become a thick purée. Continue cooking over a medium heat until the paste no longer sticks to the pan. Transfer to a bowl and mix, pressing all over with a fork or the back of a spoon to ensure that it is of an even consistency, and leave to cool. Then refrigerate for a good hour.
2 Have ready a couple of dozen paper petit four cases, a pastry board and a small bowl containing a little orange flower water, which you use to moisten your hands as you shape the sweets. Spread granulated sugar over the board. Take marble-sized pieces of mixture, form them with your damp hands into smooth balls, and roll them in sugar to give them a sparkling coating. Put each ball into a case as soon as it is made. You will need to damp your hands often, as the paste is very sticky.
3 Leave the sweets uncovered in the refrigerator to dry out for 2 to 3 days.

As an alternative, roll the balls in roughly chopped roasted almonds.

> SERVING BISCUITS, COOKIES AND PETITS FOURS AS SWEETMEATS
> All the above, which can be defined as biscuits, cookies or *petits fours*, are generally offered to guests with Turkish coffee and a glass of ice cold water, not usually as a dessert but at any time of the day. Each family will have a selection stored in separate tins in a cool place.

Left to right Basbousa, Baklava, Apricot Petits Fours and Konafa baked in a dish

BASBOUSA

PREPARATION TIME
1 hour, including cooking

MAKES 2 DOZEN SLICES

SYRUP
150 g [5 oz] sugar
juice of $\frac{1}{2}$ lemon
15 ml [1 tbsp] orange flower water
1$\frac{1}{2}$ teacupfuls water

350 g [12 oz] semolina
60 g [1 oz] desiccated coconut
100 g [3$\frac{1}{2}$ oz] vanilla sugar
10 ml [2 tsp] baking powder
1 size 2 [large] egg
300 ml [10 fl oz] natural yoghurt
30 ml [2 tbsp] milk
250 g [or 8 oz] melted butter
60–80 g [2–3 oz] whole peeled almonds

There are a thousand and one variants of these semolina slices. This is my latest version, made with natural yoghurt and flavoured with coconut.

1 Boil the ingredients for the syrup together with 1$\frac{1}{2}$ cupfuls of water until the consistency is just sticky and leave to cool.

2 Mix the semolina, coconut, vanilla sugar and baking powder in a mixing bowl. Separate the egg, reserving the white. Beat the yolk lightly. Make a well in the centre of the dry ingredients and pour in the yoghurt, milk, egg yolk and most of the melted butter (reserve enough to butter a dish generously). Mix well and beat till smooth. Beat the egg white until not quite stiff – and fold into the mixture.

3 Preheat the oven to fairly hot, 190°C [375°F, gas 5]. Butter a square or rectangular ovenproof dish about 5 cm [2 in.] deep and large enough for the mixture to about half fill it. Pour the mixture into the dish and spread it out evenly with a damp spatula. Gently tap the side of the dish to level it. Bake for 30 minutes.

4 Take the dish out of the oven and use a sharp, wetted knife to score the surface of the mixture with lengthways, then diagonal lines 3 to 4 cm [1$\frac{1}{4}$ to 1$\frac{1}{2}$ in.] apart to divide it into diamonds. Slowly pour half the syrup all over the mixture and stick an almond pointed end down into each diamond. Return to the oven for another 30 minutes.

5 Remove from the oven, pour on the rest of the syrup and leave to cool. Wet the knife and cut along the scored lines the whole way through. Carefully transfer the pieces to a serving dish to cool.

129

BAKLAVA

PREPARATION TIME
2¾ hours, including cooking
   and 1 hour cooling

MAKES 2 DOZEN SLICES

SYRUP
240 g [8 oz] **sugar**
120 ml [4 oz] **water**
lime or lemon juice
15 ml [1 tbsp] **orange flower
   water**

230 g [8 oz] **fila pastry**
230 g [8 oz] **pistachio nuts
   (weight without shells)**
60 g [2 oz] **sugar**
15 ml [1 tbsp] **orange flower
   water**
200 g [7 oz] **clarified butter, or
   half butter and half oil**

(picture on page 129)

This sumptuously rich pastry is the most universally popular of all the sweet dishes of the Middle East. However, some people consider it oversweet and soggy. I agree; but this is simply because of the enormous quantity of syrup or honey that is usually poured over it, and can therefore easily be remedied. I make a crunchier, much less sweet version. Baklava recipes vary, but in all of them fila pastry layers are filled with a nut mixture or a thick cream and baked. Then a cold thick syrup is poured over and left to soak in. From the wide range of fillings, the following one with pistachios is my favourite; it is also one of the most extravagant.

1 Make a thick syrup with the sugar, water and a squeeze of lime or lemon juice. Boil it until it reaches the thread stage: that is, when you spoon a drop of syrup on to a plate and let it cool, and then pick it up between your finger and thumb and separate them, it pulls out into a sticky thread. (If you use a sugar thermometer, it shows 110°C [230°F] at this point.) Add orange flower water and let the syrup cool completely before using it. The cooled syrup should be fairly thick, because it must not soak straight through the finished baklava, but seep in gradually.

2 Take the fila pastry out of its packet and cover it with damp cloths to keep it pliable (see below). Make the filling by roasting, shelling and coarsely grinding the nuts, and mixing them with the sugar and orange flower water. Preheat the oven to moderate, 180°C [350°F, gas 4].

3 Take a high-sided baking dish: the ideal size for this recipe is 32 × 22 × 6 cm deep [13 × 8½ × 2½ in.], and it should not be non-stick because the coating would get scratched when cutting the baklava. Melt the butter and add the oil if using both. Brush it over the dish, including the sides. Lay half the fila pastry, one sheet at a time, all over the bottom of the dish. Remember to brush the top of each sheet with butter before adding the next. The whole of the sheet must be lightly buttered. I prefer to do this with my fingers to ensure that I get the amount right. It doesn't matter if the size of the fila sheets doesn't correspond to that of your baking dish, because you can cut, overlap and patch them as necessary.

4 Spread the nut mixture evenly over the fila, then add the rest of the fila sheets in the same way as before. Take a very sharp knife or a razor blade and cut through the top few layers of fila, dividing them into diamonds about 5 × 3 cm [2 × 1 in.]. There should be a couple of dozen pieces. Then sprinkle the top with water; I find a plant spray useful for this. Put the dish on a baking sheet and bake for about 30 minutes. Then raise the heat to hot, 220°C [425°F, gas 7] for another 30 minutes or until golden brown. Pour the syrup slowly all over the baklava and leave it to cool.

* Baklava can be prepared in advance and frozen either after the first half hour's baking (thaw before continuing to bake) or when completely baked but before adding syrup.

5 Use a very sharp knife to cut right through the baklava along the scored lines. Make sure the pieces are completely separated. Transfer to a serving dish to cool.

Another filling I like is a mixture of roasted almonds, hazelnuts and walnuts with sugar, flavoured with the juice and grated zest of a small tangerine. The recipe can also be used to make individual finger shapes on the principle of borek (see pages 32–5), which can be baked or fried in the same way. If they are fried, use very little butter and don't brush the finished pastry with it.

KEEPING FILA PASTRY PLIABLE

Take the packet of fila out of the refrigerator about 30 minutes before use. Open the packet but do not unroll or separate the sheets. Cover them with a soaked and well wrung-out tea towel, draping this over two cups, one placed at each end of the roll of fila so that the damp towel does not touch it. When you are ready to use the pastry, unroll just enough to cut off what you need. If you need whole sheets, take them out one at a time and roll up the rest again. Put it back under the towel straight away. If the pastry does dry up, you will still be able to use it flat in large pieces. Dried-up offcuts of fila can also be used to make bases for tartlets (see page 28) or even for larger quiches and pies.

INDIVIDUAL KONAFA AND KONAFA BAKED IN A DISH

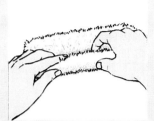

Individual Konafa

1 Unroll the defrosted konafa and take a thin layer about 30cm (12 in.) long.

2 Spoon about half the melted butter thinly all over the konafa, then spread a strip of nut filling along one long edge.

3 Gently roll the konafa over the filling to make a tight sausage shape.

4 Twist the roll from each end to give a rope effect and pour the rest of the melted butter over the top.

Konafa Baked in a Dish

1 Put the defrosted konafa in the largest mixing bowl you have and pour some of the melted butter over it.

2 Start pulling and tearing the konafa to mix it well with the melted butter. Keep turning it over and pulling and tearing, gradually adding more melted butter until it has all been added and the konafa is yellow and soft all over.

3 Line an ovenproof dish with half of the konafa. Spoon the filling evenly all over it.

4 Cover the filling with the rest of the konafa in batches. Take as much as you can handle at one time and spread it out evenly on your hand before laying it on top of the filling. Repeat until the whole dish is covered with an even layer.

KONAFA

PREPARATION TIME
2–2¼ hours, including cooking and 1 hour cooling

SERVES 8

SYRUP
240 g [8 oz] **sugar**
120 ml [4 fl oz] **water**
lime or lemon juice
15 ml [1 tbsp] **orange flower water**

CUSTARD
45 ml [3 tbsp] **ground rice**
1 litre [1¾ pints] **milk**
140 ml [5 fl oz] **double cream**
15 ml [1 tbsp] **vanilla sugar or**
1 ml [⅛ tsp] **crushed mastic**

450 g [1 lb] **konafa pastry**
230 g [8 oz] **butter, or half butter and half oil**
chopped pistachio nuts

(picture on page 129)

Konafa or 'katafi' is the partner of fila, the other great Middle Eastern pastry. Like fila, it is made with just flour and water, and needs butter added to it when it is made up. But while fila looks like sheets of paper, konafa looks like white shredded wheat. It is used in various ways, either as a pastry base and topping for a nut or cream filling, with syrup poured over, or to make small, individual confections (follow the step-by-step instructions above).

1 Prepare a syrup as for Baklava (see opposite) and allow it to cool. Also make a custard using the method for Mehalabeya (see page 122) but with the richer ingredients given here. Flavour it with mastic or vanilla sugar. Let the custard cool completely; it should be firm enough to keep its shape when you spoon it.

2 Preheat the oven to moderate, 180°C [350°F, gas 4]. Prepare the konafa with melted butter or butter and oil, following the step-by-step instructions above, and use half of it to line a deep, ovenproof dish – either one smart enough to serve it in, or a cake tin with a removable base so that you can take the finished pastry out to serve it. Pour the custard evenly over it, then spread the rest of the konafa on top and pour any remaining melted butter all over the surface. Bake for about 40 minutes, then turn up the heat to 200 or 220°C [400 or 425°F, gas 6 or 7] and bake for another 15 minutes, or until golden brown.

* Konafa can be prepared in advance to this point and frozen. Let it thaw, then give it a few minutes in a hot oven to make it crisp again before pouring on the syrup.

3 Pour the cold syrup over the konafa. Sprinkle with chopped pistachio nuts and leave to cool before serving. Use a sharp knife to cut slices.

Instead of the cream filling here, you can use a nut filling as for Baklava, both for this large dish and for individual pastries.

BREADS

I have always been a bread addict, so the recent news from nutritionists that bread is no longer sinful delights me. In my youth in Egypt my favourite bread by far was *eish baladi*, literally 'country bread'; in the recipe on page 134 I call it Arabic Bread. It is a flat, round, brown pitta-like loaf. After a lot of trial, error and perseverance I have managed to reproduce it as closely as possible with different flours and ovens.

Of course, in Egypt there was a great variety of other breads available: rings covered with sesame seeds, always fresh and crusty, which one bought in the street with a small packet of *do'a* (see page 140); the plaited loaf decorated with coloured eggs that our Greek baker used to present to us at Easter; Vienna and French loaves and bridge rolls. There was also a cylindrical brown loaf which my mother used to hollow out to insert a savoury stuffing. She would put it in the refrigerator, then slice it into neat circles revealing exciting fillings – of tuna, olives and gherkins, or ham, eggs and cheese.

ALGERIAN BREAD

This is a spiced semolina loaf.

PREPARATION TIME
2 hours 20–50 minutes,
including 1–1½ hours rising
and 45 minutes cooking

MAKES 1 LARGE LOAF

15 g [½ oz] fresh or 8 g [¼ oz, 1½ tsp] dried yeast
a pinch sugar
280 ml [10 fl oz] lukewarm water
10 ml [2 tsp] ground cinnamon
15 ml [1 tbsp] caraway seed
30 ml [2 tbsp] sesame seeds
450 g [1 lb] fine semolina
25 g [1 oz] butter + more to grease tin
1 egg
30 ml [2 tbsp] oil

1 Dissolve the yeast in a cup with the sugar and some of the measured water, stirring well. Leave it in a warm place to froth up.
2 Mix the ground cinnamon, caraway and sesame seeds with the semolina. Put the mixture on a board and make a well in the centre.
3 Melt the butter. Beat the egg and pour it into the well, add the oil, then the melted butter and the yeast mixture. Mix with the semolina to make a dough. Add water a little at a time until the dough is a little stickier than for ordinary bread, but still holding together. The quantity given is only a rough guide – use more or less as necessary. If you are using a food processor, or electric mixer, mix all the dry ingredients, turn the machine on and add the rest, leaving the water until the end.
4 Knead the dough well for at least 15 minutes.
5 Butter a large loaf tin and put in the dough. Cover it with a plastic bag and leave to rise in a warm place for 1 to 1½ hours, until it has doubled in size. This loaf does not need a second rising. When it is nearly ready, preheat the oven to hot, 230°C [450°F, gas 8].
6 Bake for about 45 minutes. Turn the loaf out, wait for a few seconds and tap the bottom, which will sound hollow if it is done. If it sounds dull, return the loaf to the oven upside down for a few more minutes. Leave the bread to cool before cutting it.

OPPOSITE Home-baked breads surrounded by loaves, bread sticks and pitta breads from the huge variety available in delicatessens and Middle Eastern shops. The Algerian Bread under the rack, Olive and Cheese Baps on the plate and flat rounds of Arabic Bread on their right are made from recipes in this chapter. LEFT Shaped loaves topped with sesame seeds, chickpeas and nuts in the window of an Israeli baker's shop.

ARABIC BREAD

PREPARATION TIME
3 hours, including 2 hours
rising and 30 minutes
cooking

MAKES ABOUT 7 ROUNDS

5 ml [1 tsp] **sugar**
285 ml [½ pint] **warm water**
45 g [1½ oz] **active dried yeast**
255 g [9 oz] **wholemeal wheat
flour**
85 g [3 oz] **strong white wheat
flour**
115 g [4 oz] **light rye flour**
15 ml [1 tbsp] **salt**
2.5 ml [½ tsp] **ground cumin
seed**
15 ml [1 tbsp] **oil**
bran

(picture on page 133)

This glorious, mottled bread brings back vivid memories of my childhood. It has taken me a long time to get close to the 'eish baladi' of which I was so fond when I was young, but now I have nearly perfected it. I managed it in different stages: first by making wholemeal pitta bread, then by adding the rye flour. Later I remembered the bran sticking at the bottom of the loaf. But the distinctive mottled brown patches were still missing. Then I hit on the idea of cooking the bread under a pre-heated grill instead of baking it in the oven. Yet I am still not quite there. There is another bread sold in Egypt, which is puffy, with a soft base and a crisp top that remain so even when the bread is cold. These I have not yet managed.

1 Dissolve the sugar in ½ cupful of the warm water. Stir in the yeast: it will dissolve without forming a clogged lump if you move the spoon to and fro instead of round and round. Leave in a warm place, and warm a large mixing bowl at the same time.

2 Tip the flour into the bowl. Add the salt and ground cumin seed, and mix well. Pour in the dissolved yeast, then the rest of the water, using some to rinse out the yeast cup. Knead for 10 to 15 minutes, if you are doing it by hand, until the dough is smooth and elastic and leaves your hands clean. If you are using a mixer or food processor, put in the dry ingredients, start the machine, then gradually pour in first the yeast mixture, then the water. When the dough has left the sides and formed a mass around the dough hook or processor blade, take it out and knead by hand for a couple of minutes to achieve a smooth, even ball of dough.

3 Remove the dough and pour the oil into the mixing bowl. Roll the dough in the oil to cover it evenly. Slip a large clear plastic bag over the bowl, folding it underneath to retain warmth and moisture. Leave in a warm place for about 2 hours or until the dough has doubled in size.

4 Heat the grill of your cooker to maximum, remove the grill rack and put the grill pan as close to the source of heat as possible. Spread some bran on an ordinary large tray and leave it on top of the stove or somewhere warm. Knead the dough well and divide it into about 7 equal-sized pieces. Take one piece at a time, knead it in your hand and flatten it into a tidy disc with your palm. Roll it into a circle about 20 cm [8 in.] across. This takes practice, but don't worry too much: the shape will improve with each piece you make, and anyway, it will still taste delicious. After shaping each round, put it on the tray of bran. By the time the tray is full the first round will be ready to cook.

5 Cook one round at a time, or as many as your grill pan will take. Slip a spatula under the round and gently transfer it to the hot grill pan. If your grill has a door which will shut with the grill pan in place, shut it. The round will take about 4 minutes to cook. (Meanwhile, roll another.) When the round is puffy and moderately browned, take it out and put it on a cooling rack.

* If you can keep yourself from eating all the bread at once, leave it to cool completely, stack it in a plastic bag, seal and store in the refrigerator or freezer. When you want to eat it, turn the grill to maximum as before, take out the bread (there is no need to thaw) and grill it with the other, paler side up for about 1 minute. With luck it should puff up again to some extent; in any case, it will still be delicious.

PITTA BREAD This is made in much the same way, but with all white or a mixture of white and wholemeal flour. The loaves are small and either round or oblong. They are usually baked on preheated baking sheets in a very hot oven, for as little as 3 to 5 minutes.

Freshly baked bread from a tanour, or clay and brick oven. Villages often have a communal oven in which each family's bread, cakes and stews can be baked on a rota system.

OLIVE AND CHEESE BAPS

PREPARATION TIME
3 hours 45 minutes, including 2 hours rising, 1 hour proving and 15 minutes cooking

MAKES 6–7 BAPS

5 ml [1 tsp] sugar
300 ml [10 fl oz] warm water
8 ml [1½ tsp] dried active yeast
300 g [10 oz] white flour
300 g [10 oz] wholemeal flour
15 ml [1 tbsp] salt
about 12 stoned olives
180 g [6 oz] halumi cheese, or dry Cheddar
30–60 ml [2–4 tbsp] olive oil

(picture on page 133)

In Cyprus they make loaves filled with olives or halumi cheese, which inspired me to make these smaller versions. I like to prepare the dough the evening before and leave it to rise overnight. If you do this, use the amount of flour given in the ingredients list, and leave the dough in a cool place. For faster rising in a warm place use only 450 g [1 lb] of flour with the same amount of yeast, water, salt etc.

1 Follow the previous recipe for Arabic Bread to the end of the rising (step 3).
2 Roughly chop the olives and cut the cheese into slices. Knead the dough well. Cut it into 6 or 7 pieces. Oil your hands with the olive oil. Knead each piece thoroughly and form it into a smooth ball. Flatten it until it is about 10 cm [4 in.] across and 1 to 1.5 cm [⅜ to ⅝ in.] thick. Use a very sharp knife to cut each bap in half horizontally, like a hamburger bun. Fill with olives and cheese. Close the halves around the filling, pinching the edges. Leave the baps in a warm place to prove for about 1 hour.
3 Preheat the oven to hot, 230°C [450°F, gas 8]. Bake the baps for about 15 minutes – check after 10 minutes. They are delicious eaten warm as a snack. Or they can be left to cool, frozen, and reheated, wrapped in foil, straight from the freezer; or simply left to thaw without reheating.

135

SAUCES AND PRESERVES

The Middle East boasts a great number of sauces to accompany and enliven simply cooked dishes such as fried fish, grilled or roast meats, pilaf and plain or stuffed vegetables. The simplest of these is a good thick natural yoghurt, which may be flavoured with garlic, onion or mint. Some, such as Tahina Dip, Hummus Dip and Babaghanoush (see pages 16 and 19) you will find in the *mezze* chapter. There is a further selection below. In general, these sauces have a mayonnaise consistency, even though most of them are not made with eggs.

I am also giving three recipes for basic sauces which form part of a number of dishes both in this book and elsewhere.

EGG AND LEMON SAUCE

PREPARATION TIME
10–15 minutes, including cooking

200 ml [7 fl oz] stock or vegetable water
15 ml [1 tbsp] cornflour
2 eggs
juice of 1–2 lemons
salt if needed

This sauce can be made with meat, chicken or fish stock according to the dish it is to accompany. It can also be poured over stuffed vegetables (see pages 92–95); if so, make it with the cooking liquid from the vegetables.

1 Heat the stock in a saucepan. In a separate bowl, dissolve the cornflour with a little stock. Whisk the eggs with the cornflour mixture until frothy but not stiff, then gradually add the lemon juice. Beat in 3 tablespoonfuls of hot stock one at a time.
2 Pour the mixture into a saucepan and keep whisking it until the sauce thickens. Be careful not to let it boil. Taste, and add salt or more lemon juice if needed. It should be the consistency of double cream. Serve hot or cold.

ZEMINO

PREPARATION TIME
20–25 minutes, including 10–15 minutes cooking

2 cloves garlic
30 ml [2 tbsp] dry breadcrumbs
1 small can anchovy fillets
15 ml [1 tbsp] oil
15 ml [1 tbsp] tomato purée
½ teacupful water
15–30 ml [1–2 tbsp] vinegar, to taste
about 5 ml [1 tsp] sugar

We always had this anchovy and vinegar sauce with fried fish at home, but I am not sure of its origin. I've never had it anywhere else, either in Egypt or since we left. Even the name is a puzzle, for it does not seem to come from any language I know.

1 Crush the garlic with the breadcrumbs in a pestle and mortar (or a food processor), working them together until completely blended. Add the anchovies and keep blending until you get a smooth purée.
2 Gently fry the purée in oil on a low heat until you can smell the fragrance of cooked garlic. Stir in the tomato purée. Add ½ teacupful of water, then the vinegar, stirring all the time. Taste, and add as much more vinegar as you judge right, and also a little sugar. Keep cooking on a low heat, still stirring constantly, until you get a thick sauce. Serve cold.

TRAHANAS SAUCE

PREPARATION TIME
2–3 hours soaking
10 minutes

120 g [4 oz] trahanas
2 cloves garlic
salt to taste
stock (optional)

Since I discovered trahanas and found it so delicious, I have experimented with using it in all kinds of ways. I have devised this sauce, which makes a fine accompaniment to grilled meat or fish, or to stuffed vegetables.

1 Put the trahanas in a bowl, just cover with water and leave to soak for a few hours.
2 Squash it with a fork until it has the consistency of porridge. Strain through a sieve and reserve the liquid. Crush the garlic with salt and mix it well with a little of the trahanas paste. Add the remaining paste and mix well. This makes a splendid cold sauce.

For a hot, more liquid sauce, heat it gently, stirring all the time and adding some of the reserved soaking liquid (or any kind of stock, if you prefer) to give the right consistency; it should be like a rather grainy mayonnaise. Watch that it doesn't stick to the pan.

GARLIC SAUCE

PREPARATION TIME
30–40 minutes, including 25
    minutes cooking

about 250 g [or 8 oz] potatoes
2 cloves garlic
salt to taste
juice of 1–2 limes or lemons
about 120 ml [4 fl oz] oil

In our Sephardic family we called this sauce 'ajada' – from 'ajo', Spanish for garlic. In Spain itself you find a similar sauce called 'patatas al ajillo'; and the Skordalia below is another of the same type from Greece. Garlic sauces can be made with potatoes or bread. There must be as many versions as there are cooks who make them. Mine is inspired by the memory of one made by a neighbour in Cairo who originally came from Corfu. It has the consistency of mayonnaise.

1 Boil and peel the potatoes. Crush the garlic to a paste with a little salt.
2 If you are using a pestle and mortar (which must be large), add the potatoes a chunk at a time and blend well. Add more salt and a little lime or lemon juice gradually, then very slowly trickle in the oil, beating all the time. When the mixture has the right consistency, taste it and adjust the seasoning. If using a food processor or blender, blend the garlic with a bit of potato first, so that you start with a smooth, even mixture. Then add the remaining ingredients in the same order.

SKORDALIA Use about 120 g [or 4 oz] of soft breadcrumbs instead of potatoes. Vinegar is often used instead of lemon juice, and sometimes ground almonds are added. For obvious reasons, the final sauce is not as smooth as the one made with potatoes. It looks very similar to Trahanas Sauce (see opposite), but has a pungent sharpness rather than the milder burghul and yoghurt flavour or trahanas.

TOMATO SAUCE

PREPARATION TIME
30–40 minutes, including
    cooking

2 large onions
2 cloves garlic
30 ml [2 tbsp] oil
500 g [or 1 lb] tomatoes or
400 g [14 oz] can tomatoes
45 ml [3 tbsp] chopped parsley
30 ml [2 tbsp] tomato purée
a strip lemon peel
salt and pepper to taste

1 Grate or very finely chop the onions and garlic and put in a heavy-based pan with the oil. Cook over medium heat for about 10 minutes. Skin the tomatoes and discard any watery bits if using fresh ones. Drain canned tomatoes.
2 Add the parsley, tomatoes and the tomato purée. Squash and mix everything with a wooden spoon. Add a strip of lemon peel, salt and pepper. Leave to cook, uncovered, on medium heat for a further 20 to 30 minutes, stirring occasionally, until the ingredients blend into a rich sauce.
* This sauce is ideal for storing in the freezer. I usually omit any extra flavouring so that I can add whatever is appropriate when I come to use it.

The seasoning and flavour of this sauce can be varied endlessly. You can use one, two or more of the following: ginger, saffron or turmeric, cumin, coriander (leaf or seed), allspice, thyme, basil, mint, oregano . . . the important thing is that no single flavour is overpowering. You can also add some grated carrots or very finely chopped celery when the onions are cooked (step 1).

MEAT AND TOMATO SAUCE

PREPARATION TIME
30–40 minutes, including
    cooking

15–30 ml [1–2 tbsp] olive oil
1 large onion
2 cloves garlic
45 ml [3 tbsp] chopped parsley
250 g [8 oz] lean beef or lamb,
    minced or cut into cubes
1 400 g [14 oz] can tomatoes
15 ml [1 tbsp] tomato purée
salt and pepper to taste
a pinch thyme
1 bay leaf

The secret of a good sauce is to cook it until there is no taste of water; the ability to recognize this comes through experience. Taste after, say, 10 minutes cooking and again when the sauce is beginning to thicken. The difference will be obvious. When I get students to do this, they often ask what I have added because the flavour is so greatly improved.

1 Take a heavy-based pan and pour in enough olive oil to just coat the bottom. Grate or finely chop the onion, add to the pan and set it over medium heat. Cook until the onion is soft and transparent. Chop the garlic finely.
2 Increase the heat and stir until the onion begins to brown. Then add the finely chopped garlic, the chopped parsley and the meat, and stir until the meat is evenly browned. Drain the tomatoes, reserving the liquid, and add them with the tomato purée, salt, pepper, thyme and bay leaf. Bring to simmering point, half cover the pan and cook on a low heat for 20 to 30 minutes, stirring from time to time. If the sauce dries up or sticks, scrape the pan and add some liquid from the can, or water. Taste and adjust the seasoning.

Sauces and preserves (*left to right*) Egg and Lemon, Zemino, Trahanas and Garlic sauces. In the jars: pink Pickled Turnips, Preserved Lemons and bought mixed pickles

BÉCHAMEL SAUCE

PREPARATION TIME
20 minutes, including cooking

30 g [1 oz] **butter**
25 ml [1 heaped tbsp] **flour**
500 ml [or 1 pint] **milk**
salt and pepper to taste

This plain white sauce is one of the simplest basic sauces, used in Middle Eastern as well as European cooking, yet it often looks and tastes awful. It takes some patience to make it well: unctuous, free from lumps and, above all, fully cooked so that it does not taste of raw flour or cling to the palate. Whatever method you use, it will take a good 20 minutes to achieve a satisfactory result.

1 Melt the butter over a low heat in a heavy-based saucepan. As soon as it has all melted, add the flour and stir vigorously, keeping the heat low.
2 Add the milk very gradually – no more than a couple of tablespoonfuls at a time. Mix thoroughly and do not neglect the sides of the pan. As soon as each addition is blended smoothly, add a little more milk. As the sauce thickens, it is often necessary to take it off the heat while you add the next lot of milk. Eliminate any lumps as soon as they form by vigorous stirring. Ensure that the heat is low enough to keep the mixture from colouring or sticking to the base of the pan. Carry on until you have added about three-quarters of the milk, stirring hard all the time.
3 Taste the sauce. If you can detect any taste of raw flour, don't increase the heat, but keep adding milk slowly. As soon as the sauce tastes properly cooked, stir in any remaining milk in one lot. Let the sauce cook until it reaches the required consistency, stirring frequently and making sure that it doesn't stick to the sides and bottom of the pan. Season with salt, pepper and whatever else is required for the particular dish.

PICKLED TURNIPS

PREPARATION TIME
30 minutes
14 days wait

MAKES 1 KG [2 LB] PICKLES

450 g [1 lb] turnips
1 raw beetroot
about 12 allspice berries
salt: 80 g ordinary salt or 55 g
    sea salt per litre water [3 tbsp
    ordinary or 2 tbsp sea salt
    per pint]

All kinds of vegetables can be pickled. Cucumbers, turnips and cabbage are my favourites, and I like them in brine rather than in vinegar. Small 'Cyprus' type cucumbers, now increasingly easy to get in this country, are the ones found in the Middle East. However, it is cheaper and quicker to buy them ready pickled: excellent ones in brine are imported from Poland and Israel; the Israeli ones are especially small and delicate. Pickled turnips are not widely sold here, but they are easy to make yourself. The turnips must be submerged all the time, but they tend to float in the brine. There are various ways of keeping them down. The first is to use a smooth, flat, well-scrubbed stone. The method I find easier is to clean and use a jar small enough to fit inside each larger jar.

1 Make sure your preserving jar (or jars) and utensils are all absolutely clean: use one of the proprietary sterilizers for babies' bottles or home winemaking equipment.
2 Wash and scrub the turnips. Top, tail and halve them. If using large turnips, peel, slice and cut them into fingers. Wash, peel and slice the beetroot. Put the turnips in the jar, or jars, with slices of beetroot and whole allspice berries in between them.
3 Fill a pan with at least enough water to cover the vegetables: this will be a good 600 ml [over 1 pint] for the quantities given here. Add the necessary amount of salt: you will need less sea salt than ordinary salt because it has a stronger flavour. Bring the brine to the boil, then let it cool for a minute or so and pour over the turnips. Press the turnips down with a smooth flat stone or a small jar of suitable size so that when the lid is on, they will be completely submerged.
4 Seal and leave in a warm place for about two weeks before using. Once you have opened a jar, it should be kept in the refrigerator.

The beetroot is not necessary, but it gives the pickle a lovely pink colour.

PICKLED CAULIFLOWER Cut the cauliflower into florets and treat as above.

PICKLED CABBAGE Shred the cabbage thickly and treat as above, taking particular care to keep it all submerged.

All these pickles are very good without any further flavouring, but often a clove of garlic or a few celery leaves are added with the vegetables or brine (step 2 or 3).

PRESERVED LEMONS OR LIMES

PREPARATION TIME
30 minutes, including 2–3
    minutes cooking
10–14 days wait

8–10 lemons or limes
5 ml [1 tsp] salt for each fruit +
    one for the jar

Preserved lemons or limes add a sharp flavour and make a decorative addition to the 'mezze' table. Rinsed and cut into small strips, they may be added to an hors d'oeuvre dish with black olives and small cubes of feta cheese, and sprinkled with a little olive oil. They are added to a number of stews and salads, and can also be served as you would any pickle. Choose small, juicy, thin-skinned fruit. Use a wide-mouthed 1 kg [2 lb] preserving jar.

1 Wash and scrub the fruit thoroughly. Boil some water in a large saucepan. Use a little to rinse the preserving jar and its seal, and leave them to drain dry without wiping. Put the fruit into the boiling water for 2 to 3 minutes, then remove and plunge into cold water.
2 Sprinkle about a teaspoonful of salt over the bottom of the jar. Cut all but two of the fruit almost in quarters from one end, leaving the pieces just joined, and prise out the pips. Do this over a plate to catch the juice. Put a teaspoonful of salt into each fruit. Pack tightly into the jar, pressing each layer down hard before adding the next.
3 Slice one of the remaining fruits, put the slices in the top of the jar and sprinkle it with a teaspoonful of salt. Squeeze the juice from the last one and pour into the jar. Sprinkle the last teaspoonful of salt into the two squeezed halves and put them, peel upward, on top of the slices.
4 Squeeze everything down as hard as you can with a spoon to release more juice, so that it covers the fruit. Then weight them down to keep them from floating.
5 Keep in a warm place for 10 to 14 days. The slices will be ready to use before the larger pieces. To test if they are ready, cut a piece off one with a fork. If it cuts easily, rinse it and taste: it should have no bitterness but a refreshing sourness.

CONDIMENTS

Mixed condiments are often added to soups, stews and sauces. There are many different mixtures and ways of preparing them.

DO'A

This is a general term for various mixtures of nuts, seeds, spices or herbs, eaten with bread – either flat Arabic Bread (see page 134) or sesame-seed rings or sticks. Making some kinds of *do'a* used to be a long and tedious job, but now you can do it in a flash with a food processor or liquidizer. Here are two recipes.

Sesame and coriander do'a This is by far my favourite. Take 250 g [or 8 oz] of sesame seeds and 60 g [2 oz] of coriander seed and pick over both carefully, removing any stones or foreign bodies. Dry roast the sesame seeds, stirring constantly to avoid burning, until they are light brown, and set aside. Do the same with the coriander. Put the coriander into the machine first and pulverize it, then add the sesame seeds. Stop as soon as the texture is sandy, or the sesame seeds will turn into a paste. This would be all right if you were planning to use it right away – you could spread it on your bread like peanut butter. But if you want it to keep, it must remain dry or it will go rancid. Tip the mixture into a bowl, add salt to taste and mix well.

Every time I make this I get a slightly different result, depending mainly on the length of time I roast the ingredients. The proportions can be varied, but don't use more than one-third coriander or the mixture will be too bitter. You can also add a few roasted hazelnuts.

Herb do'a This is a popular mixture: we used to buy little packets of it in the street to eat with sesame bread rings. It is also delicious with hard-boiled eggs. Simply mix salt, pepper and crushed dried mint in the proportions 1:2:3. Instead of mint, *za'atar* (wild thyme) is also used; you could try it with any kind of thyme. A slice of good home-made bread moistened with olive oil and sprinkled with this *do'a* makes a splendid snack.

HARISSA

In its simplest form this hot preparation consists of chillis, salt and oil. It can be bought ready-made from Middle Eastern stores as a paste in tubes, or cans; the recipes in this book assume that you will use ready-made harissa. Any plain chilli sauce, available from West Indian and Chinese shops, will serve as an alternative. However, it is easy to make your own and this allows you to add extra ingredients to make the flavour more interesting. For plain harissa, pound 100 g [3½ oz] of dried red chillis with 8 ml [1 heaped tsp] of salt. When the mixture is reduced to a fine consistency, put it in a jar and cover with oil. For a spicier mixture, use 80 g of dried red chillis, 50 g [½ oz] of garlic, 30 g [1 oz] of caraway seed and 8 ml [1 heaped tsp] of salt; pound and cover with oil as above.

TA'LEYA

This is an Egyptian favourite which is absolutely essential to some dishes, such as, for instance, Melokheya (see page 42). It is made from pounded or very finely chopped garlic fried with ground coriander and sometimes other additions. Crush 3 or 4 cloves of garlic with 15 ml [1 tbsp] of coriander seed. Fry gently in clarified butter or oil until the aroma develops, being careful not to burn it. Pour immediately into the dish to which it is to be added. Use a little liquid from this to free the last remnants of Ta'leya from the frying pan. You can add a couple of tablespoonfuls of vinegar or a touch of chilli powder to the mixture.

T'ATBIL

This is a similar mixture used in Tunisia. It invariably contains caraway seed and dried red chillis as well as the other ingredients. Traditionally a large amount is made at once: everything is pounded in a mortar, dried in the sun and sent to be ground at a mill. For making small amounts of this, or any other spice mixture, at home, a spice grinder is very useful. For 3 cloves of garlic use 10 ml [2 tsp] each of coriander and caraway seed and 1 dried red chilli. The mixture can be fried like Ta'leya, or used as it is.

A soft drinks stall in the Lebanon. The silver urns contain fruit syrups and juices, cold mint tea and perhaps pickle juices.

DRINKS

The Middle East produces some excellent wines, beer and a strong aniseed-flavoured drink known as as *ouzo*, *raki* or *arak*, which is usually diluted with water and served with some food – olives, feta cheese, or some other *mezze* dish. However, since alcohol is forbidden in many areas, it is more usual to find non-alcoholic drinks served, either with or without meals. Fresh fruit juices of all kinds are among the most popular drinks. Here is a selection of my favourite non-alcoholic drinks.

COFFEE

Coffee prepared in the universal Middle Eastern way is known as Turkish coffee in the west, but exactly the same drink is called Arabic or Greek coffee, depending on where it is served. The coffee beans are ground as fine as flour and brewed in a specially shaped pot called *ibrik* in Turkish and *kanaka* in colloquial Egyptian. Traditionally these were of copper or brass and often highly ornamental, but now plain aluminium ones are usual. They vary in size according to the number of cups they are designed to make. This varies from one to four; it is not a good idea to make larger quantities in one pot. The quantities given here are for two tiny cupfuls of medium sweet coffee.

Turkish coffee has a reputation of being over-sweet and full of muddy grounds, but there is no reason for it to be either. The coffee beans should be so finely pulverized that the powder sinks into a compact mass that stays in the bottom of the cup. Since stirring would raise the grounds, the coffee is always sweetened to the required degree when it is made.

1 Put 10 ml [2 tsp] of sugar with 2 coffee cupfuls of water in a 2 cup size *kanaka* or your narrowest small saucepan (this should almost fill it). Put the pot on to boil.
2 When the water boils, pour out about $\frac{1}{2}$ cupful and reserve. Add 18 ml [2 very heaped tsp] of coffee, a spoonful at a time, stirring vigorously after each addition until the spoon comes out clean. Put the pot back on medium heat and watch it like a hawk.
3 The moment the water boils, take the pot off the heat and tap it gently against the side of the stove. The coffee will subside, and there will be room to pour back the reserved $\frac{1}{2}$ cupful of water. Bring it back to the boil and tap it again. By now there should be a good froth on top, and the coffee is ready to serve.

For an authentic touch, serve the coffee with the pot on a tray with the two cups, two glasses of iced water and some small sweet meats, or small saucers of jam; to be eaten with a spoon. Pouring the coffee requires some care: it gets easier with practice. First tip some of the froth into a cup with a quick single movement, then pour the rest of the froth into another. Pour out the rest of the coffee slowly, so as not to spoil the froth. The greater the quantity of coffee brewed in one go, the harder it is to produce enough of the highly prized froth for everyone.

Some people add a drop of cold water to the cup before drinking their coffee, which both cools it and ensures that the grounds are quite settled at the bottom. You should stop drinking before you reach them.

Spices, especially cardamom, are sometimes added to the cold water in the pot. Use a couple of cracked pods for 2 cupfuls. Ready-ground Arabic coffee with cardamom already added is also available.

DRIED LIME TEA

This is made with dried limes, crushed and infused in boiling water for a few minutes. Use one dried lime per mugful. I prefer it unsweetened, but most people do add sugar.

DRIED LIME AND GINGER TEA

This is a marvellously warming mixture that I devised one bitterly cold evening. Dried ginger root is preferable to ready-ground or fresh ginger, though both these are adequate. For four mugfuls use two dried limes and a piece of ginger about 3 cm [1 in.] long, which will produce about 1 heaped teaspoonful of powder. (If you are using ready-ground ginger, halve this quantity.) Mix the two in a teapot, pour on boiling water and infuse for a few minutes before serving. Alter the proportions to taste.

SAHLEB DRINK

This thick, cinnamon-spiced hot milk drink is correctly made with *sahleb* or *salep*, which can be hard to get. I have invented a most acceptable alternative which I have offered to Egyptian friends who are fooled into thinking that it does contain *sahleb*. The quantities given here would make two mugfuls.

Dissolve 8 ml [1 heaped tsp] arrowroot in a couple of tablespoonfuls of milk taken from 2 mugfuls in a heavy-based saucepan and set over medium heat. Add the rest of the milk gradually, stirring all the time. Stir in a good pinch of ground cinnamon and just a pinch of crushed mastic. When it thickens slightly, pour into the mugs, add sugar to taste and sprinkle cinnamon and chopped hazelnuts or pistachios on top.

YOGHURT DRINK

This is very refreshing and simple to prepare. Dilute natural yoghurt with an equal amount of iced water (or vary the proportions to taste), and add a pinch of crushed dried mint and salt to taste if you like.

ACKNOWLEDGMENTS

My first and greatest debt of gratitude is to the people who taught me to cook: my late mother and aunt Mary; also to Ida Dolso who lived with us for some years and who first introduced me to soup with her superb minestrone (not so different from various lovely Middle Eastern soups), and who watched patiently as I took over her kitchen. I also wish to thank Lucie Farhi of Paris, who over the years acquainted me with the Syrian Jewish tradition in Egyptian cooking. She taught me to make different kinds of kibbeh, her way of using spices, and how to organize large buffet parties. Dalila and Nadja, two London friends from Algeria and Tunisia respectively, have not only introduced me to their own cuisines but have shown me how akin they are to my own. Fatima Ma'toughi, a Moroccan cook I met through friends in Paris, cooked with me for a week. She revealed all her secrets for making a perfect Pastilla and for blending herbs and spices in delicious *tajines*.

Many friends have generously provided or contributed to recipes in this book: Angèle Argi, Sonia Cohen, Vera Janković and Mireille Attas in London, Jacqueline Biancardi in Paris, Emily Amiel and Bondi Attas in Montreal, Vesna Karanović and Zagurka Cvejić in Belgrade.

I am also grateful to past students who have given me much insight into the way people read and use cookery books, and who have shown by their enthusiasm that they appreciated my unorthodox way of teaching.

I thank Weidenfeld & Nicolson, my publishers, and Marks & Spencer for not only allowing, but even encouraging me to write this book in such a personal way.

My particular thanks go to Vicky Hayward at Weidenfeld who, from behind the scenes, encouraged, and coaxed me whenever I needed it; also to my copy editor, Ralph Hancock, whose academic knowledge and meticulousness did not deter him from accepting my idiosyncrasies, and whose enthusiastic backing and advice sustained me through the most difficult periods. I also enjoyed working with Lisa Collard, who cooked for the photographs. Last but not least, my grateful admiration goes to Celia Dodd, who as the editor was in the forefront of coordinating the work of many people, all pulling and pushing in different directions, to produce what we all wanted to be a successful book.

Illustrations have been reproduced by kind permission of the following:
p.6 selling melons, Anne M. Holt/Sonia Halliday Photographs; p.7 nut harvest, Ingrid Rangnow/Zefa; p.8 Athenian Grocery, Jill Brown; p.8 Samadi's Patisserie, Jill Brown; p.9 market stall, Jill Brown; p.10 date harvest, G. Heil/Zefa; p.11 making coffee, Magnum; p.17 Yemenite market, Jane Taylor/Sonia Halliday Photographs; p.21 peppers drying, Robert Harding Picture Library; p.29 spice stall, Bernard Regent/Alan Hutchison Library; p.38 sacks of spices, Sybil Sasson/Robert Harding Picture Library; p.43 bread making, Liba Taylor/Alan Hutchison Library; p.46 fishing boats, Ian Berry/Magnum; p.56 vineyards and cone dwellings, Sonia Halliday Photographs; p.63 Berber market, Robert Harding Picture Library; p.70 butcher's shop, Jill Brown; p.80 pulses, nuts and seeds, Jane Taylor/Sonia Halliday Photographs; p.86 vegetable stall, Jill Brown/MEPhA; p.105 rice fields, Desmond Harvey/Robert Harding Picture Library; p.107 harvesting wheat, Middle East Pictures and Publicity; p.113 Turkish wheat harvest, Richard Ashworth/Robert Harding Picture Library; p.117 orange market, Sonia Halliday Photographs; p.120 market stall with dates, Gemma Levine; p.124 trays of cakes, Christina Gascoigne/Robert Harding Picture Library; p.132 baker's window, Jill Brown; p.135 village oven, Middle East Pictures and Publicity; p.143 fruit stall, Middle East Pictures and Publicity.

I would particularly like to thank Jacqueline Biancardi for her kind permission to use her recipes for Fried Chicken with Sesame Seeds (page 61) and Lamb with Pasta (page 71), both reproduced from *La Cuisine Grecque* [Ed. Jacques Grancher, Paris, 1984]. I would also like to acknowledge my indebtedness to Tess Matlos for her unique tip on soaking okra in vinegar (page 87), which comes from her *Complete Middle East Cookbook* [McGraw Hill, Toronto, 1979].

All food photography by Paul Bussell
Preparation of food for photography by Lisa Collard
Photographic stylist Penny Markham
Jacket, half title and black-and-white illustrations by Christopher Brown
Step-by-step illustrations by Edwina Keene
Jacket and chapter title lettering by Kate Cary
Design/Art Direction Sara Komar

INDEX

A Tunisian fruit stall: fresh fruit is
varied and abundant in the Middle East